Quarterly Essay

Quarterly Essay is published four times a year by Black Inc., an imprint of Schwartz Books Pty Ltd. Publisher: Morry Schwartz.

ISBN 9781760644406 ISSN 1444-884x

Subscriptions – 1 year print & digital (4 issues): $89.99 within Australia incl. GST. Outside Australia $124.99. 2 years print & digital (8 issues): $169.99 within Australia incl. GST. 1 year digital only: $59.99.

Payment may be made by Mastercard or Visa, or by cheque made out to Schwartz Books. Payment includes postage and handling.

To subscribe, fill out and post the subscription card or form inside this issue, or subscribe online:

quarterlyessay.com
subscribe@quarterlyessay.com
Phone: 61 3 9486 0288

Correspondence should be addressed to:

The Editor, Quarterly Essay
22–24 Northumberland Street
Collingwood VIC 3066 Australia
Phone: 61 3 9486 0288 / Fax: 61 3 9011 6106
Email: quarterlyessay@blackincbooks.com

Editor: Chris Feik. Management: Elisabeth Young. Publicity: Anna Lensky. Design: Guy Mirabella. Associate Editor: Kirstie Innes-Will. Production Coordinator: Marilyn de Castro. Typesetting: Typography Studio.

Printed in Australia by McPherson's Printing Group. The paper used to produce this book comes from wood grown in sustainable forests.

There may be some mistake about a doctrine which makes the wicked, when a majority, the mouthpiece of God against the virtuous, but the hopes of mankind are staked on it; and if the weak in faith sometimes quail when they see humanity floating in a shoreless ocean, on this plank, which experience and religion long since condemned as rotten, mistake or not, men have thus far floated better by its aid, than the popes ever did with their prettier principle, so that it will be a long time yet before society repents.

Henry Adams, *Democracy: An American Novel*, 1880

HIGH NOON

Trump, Harris and America on the brink

Don Watson

East of the Rocky Mountains in the American spring, moist warm air from the Gulf of Mexico and the southwest collides with cold upper-level air from the Rocky Mountains and Canada. In the chaos of contending winds and temperatures, supercell thunderstorms develop, and from the belly of their sullen black clouds a slender funnel shimmies forth. As if obeying instinct, it reaches for the ground.

More tornadoes are born in Tornado Alley than anywhere else on Earth. About 150 were reported in the second week of May this year. Some have brief lives; some career across the plains for miles. Three years ago, a tornado carved a 220-mile path through Kentucky, killing a hundred people. So far this year tornadoes have killed thirty-nine. Tornado Alley is moving into the more densely populated lands east of the Mississippi. Scientists say it's climate change: there are more tornadoes now and the season is starting earlier.

When they touch down tornadoes seem to hesitate, as if deciding where to prove that Nature is not done yet. We are human, and some of us can't help imagining they are the unnatural incarnation of vengeful or lunatic spirits, testing us or exacting retribution. Tornadoes reduce one building to sticks and rubble and spare those on either side of it. One family must find a new home; their next-door neighbours have only to get out their leaf blower and sweep a bit of debris from their drives. Other tornadoes are less selective and cut a wider swathe, destroying everything in their path. It is this mad fury and vindictiveness that leads people of faith to see the Almighty in tornadoes – or whirlwinds, as the Bible calls them. There are kinds of Calvinists in the way of America's tornadic hordes who, holding to the absolute sovereignty of God, believe with the Hebrew prophet that "the Lord cometh in the tempest, and the ways of him be in the whirlwind." As it was with Hurricane Katrina and other natural calamities, in tornado season Bibles will be opened, particularly at the Book of Job, prayers will be offered, forgiveness sought and trust in the Lord and understanding of his ways restored. And as it was with Katrina, and has always been in the American heartland, every visitation will rouse communities to faith-sustaining acts of charity and love. *That* too is how God is in the whirlwind. The whirlwind gives as it taketh away.

*

Our lives are full of entertainments, many of them senseless and alarming, and it is folly to believe that politics must not – or will not – imitate the public riot. It was a bit like this in the middle of May. By day, the courtroom drama in New York, where Donald Trump was on trial for falsifying records to hide a payoff to a porn star, the whole affair shot through with sleaze and corruption, and figures who would be improbable if we had not seen them so often in films and television shows. After a day listening to Michael Cohen (the old consigliere he now calls a "Rat") testify against him as convincingly as any professional liar could, we see him addressing a big rally in New Jersey. Then he's back in court as Stormy Daniels (an old sexual conquest he now calls "Horseface") describes spanking his bare buttocks with a rolled-up copy of *Forbes* magazine.

New Jersey has been solidly Democrat since 1988, but Trump says he'll win it, and the crowd of "hardworking patriots" cheer and chant. Never mind that Daniels has that day said of the former president, "I don't owe him shit. I'll never give that orange turd a dime"; or that his "legacy in Atlantic City [New Jersey] has long been defined by self-dealing, financial trouble, and avoiding paying small, mom-and-pop contractors," that he "stiffed many people and … made a mockery" of the town: he says he'll win New Jersey with "love, intelligence and a thing called common sense." And the "hardworking patriots" cheer and chant, "USA! USA!"

Trump has turned Republican politics, and therefore much of American politics, into the wildly adversarial and addictive world of TV wrestling, an entertainment he used to make money and forge his public persona. Back in the 1980s he staged WrestleMania at Trump Plaza Hotel and Casino in Atlantic City and made sure he was seen ringside. Too bad if a mobster was also in the shot. In truth, the wrestling was staged in a convention hall across the road from Trump Plaza, but who was going to care about that little detail? In 1988 Trump already had Hulk Hogan spruiking for him – and for the venue. In a rave to camera that Trump just might have had a hand in, Hulk told 33 million fans:

> when I get Andre the Giant … when I *slam* him through the Trump Plaza, brother, from New York down to Tampa, Florida, the faultline is gonna break off! And as Andre the Giant falls into the ocean, as my next two opponents fall to the ocean floor and I pin 'em, so will Donald Trump and all the Hulkamaniacs. But as Donald Trump hangs onto the top of the Trump Plaza, with his family under his other arm, as they sink to the bottom of the sea, thank God Donald Trump's a Hulkamaniac because he'll know enough to let go of his materialist possessions, hang on to the wife and kids, dog paddle with his life all the way to safety.

TV wrestling involves a lot of boasting, posturing and abusing, as well as body slamming. It owes something to the "sensationalism" of tabloid journalism and something to cartoons. The wrestlers are real, but not real. They are personifications of good and evil, courage and cowardice, patriotism and treachery. They are often unhinged. Despite the violence, there is no blood or bruising. Like Yosemite Sam when he's been blown to smithereens, they've no sooner been body-slammed than they get right back up again. It is a fiction, a melodrama, a parody.

But try telling TV wrestling fans that what they're watching is all a lie: see who looks silly. *Prove* it's a fake and you'll look even sillier. Try it at a Trump rally or Republican Convention. Fans enter the world of TV wrestling as they enter any other fiction, knowing it's make-believe but open to its seduction. They boo and hiss and shout, much as kids used to at Punch and Judy shows, much as we all do during elections. By making politics like TV wrestling, Trump created a fictional setting for his fictions. He can be as abusive and as untruthful as he likes. In a fictional world, to lie and keep on lying is a requirement. For some, it is also essential to be hated. You can sound demented, might even *be* demented; the more demented you are the more you blend with the environment.

*

Within a few hundred yards of the house tucked beneath the gum trees lining Sunset Boulevard, where I am pampered by my friends, live three famous late-career movie actresses and an equally admired actor and director who recently played Leonard Bernstein with a prosthetic nose. Other A-listers, or former A-listers, live nearby, as once did the Reagans and before them Will Rogers. Nowhere else in the world could we find ourselves within spitting distance of so many people we've never met but who, should we meet them walking their cavoodles or backing out their Teslas, we would recognise as we might an old friend: and in the instant before our minds have sorted real life from the parallel one created by American film and television, we might even greet them as warmly as we would a friend, as once in a Whole Foods shop I warmly greeted Andie MacDowell.

Los Angeles is only different by degree: *everywhere* in the United States, fragments of Hollywood's alternate universe flicker into view, as if one's brain contained an old projector with a faulty lamp.

Nestled among the canyons, within easy reach of the ocean, and Sunset Boulevard purring out of sight, realtors speak of Norman Rockwell, though the scene is one of such storybook beauty Wes Anderson might have designed it. The homes, in a variety of elegant twentieth-century styles, and defended by security firms that leave their names on tasteful little yard signs, sell for anything from five to sixty-five million dollars. The manicured gardens are tended by fleets of conscientious workers, Central and South American and Asian – in another context not a few of them would be called illegal immigrants.

It's all Democrat, one guesses, unless there's the odd country-club Republican in mourning for George H.W. Bush, or in the present circumstances even his limited son Dubya. My genial hosts are lifelong active Democrats: he a Yale-educated veteran of the 1960s student movement, a civic activist in Santa Monica's radical reform days, Bill Clinton adviser, US ambassador, just retired professor at Occidental (where Barack Obama studied), ultra-well-connected networker with a sure grasp of political history and contemporary strategy; she Berkeley-educated in the same era and, among other successful endeavours, the founder of a non-profit which draws hundreds of men and women from minority populations to mentor and guide them into the senior reaches of the financial industry: for which sterling enterprise she's been made an inductee of the Berkeley Women's Hall of Fame.

The way downtown snakes along a seventy-mile section of the empire's western balcony. During Prohibition, bootleggers and casino operators used to anchor their boats out there, just beyond the three-mile limit. "Los Angeles is particularly vulnerable to the destructive effects of wildfires, flooding, mudslides, earthquakes, and extreme heat," a LA city information sheet warns. Tsunamis are also possible. But the west wasn't won with faint hearts. In any event, the people of Los Angeles have always had better things to do than fret about natural disasters – like make films about them. Earthquake, fire, tsunami, meteorite strike, global warming, pandemic, tornadoes of course – *Twisters*, a sequel to the 1996 film *Twister*, has just been made. No catastrophe can defy Hollywood's ability to render it.

No monster either. Giant gorillas, gelatinous blobs, phenomenal sharks, rebarbative aliens, bloodsuckers, insatiable carnivores, horrible insectoids, terminators, Things that eat you. Every dark mental abyss given legs and teeth, and an American hero or antihero to deal with it. Dix Steele, the serial killer in Dorothy B. Hughes' *In a Lonely Place*, cruised this foreshore on balmy evenings, looking for women to strangle. Humphrey Bogart later immortalised and sanitised him. Beginning with Charlie Chaplin in 1914, hundreds of movies and TV series have set scenes on Santa Monica pier. Philip Marlowe, Raymond Chandler's private detective, paid a visit to the pier in *Farewell, My Lovely*. He was on his way to settle some business with Moose Molloy and Moose's faithless girlfriend on one of those shady boozing and gambling boats.

The private detective, Chandler said, was "a complete man and a common man and yet an unusual man." Uncommon perhaps because he sits somewhere between Americans' reverence for the law ("in America the law is king," Tom Paine said) and their high regard for *lawbreakers*, those who are a law unto themselves – from the likes of Jesus Christ to the founders to Walt Whitman (Americans "think lightly of the laws," he said) to you name it … *Thelma and Louise*. The popular culture and the founding documents indicate that the rule of law and freedom from it are equally esteemed. Chandler's uncommon man has little time for laws or lawyers, and only a little more for police – his beat is between people of good character (or good enough) and creeps: "down these mean streets a man must go who is not himself mean, who is neither tarnished nor afraid."

Between them, Chandler, Hughes, Dashiell Hammett and a few dozen other writers and filmmakers came up with the whole waxworks of bad actors: chancers, confidence men, hitmen, crooked cops, corrupt politicians and public officials, expropriators, sleaze merchants, mobsters, perverts, pretty boys, pimps, prostitutes, pornographers, parasites, gun molls, tramps, temptresses, cokeheads, debauchees, desperadoes, hucksters, grifters, lowlifes, thieves, suckers. Take a rough half-dozen of them and massage them into a decent suit and you have something like Donald Trump. The quest is to find a Philip Marlowe to bring him down.

Trump's supporters see him differently, of course. Among the several bodies the former US president represents – the nation, the government, the executive, the party – the hardest to read is the body of people who voted for him. American liberals – and liberals all over the world – find it beyond understanding that *anyone* could vote for this rapist, crook, vulgarian, liar, FELON. This "vile" person, as Nancy Pelosi called him.

As if mesmerised by his awfulness, perhaps too often they rail against him, rather than *for* the hard core of Americans whose alienation and despair leave them open to his predations. But the Democrats lost these people eight years ago, when Trump stoked the embers of their resentment, their sense of betrayal and abandonment, their loneliness, their suspicions, their belief that folk like them carry more of the burden, including the military burden, only to suffer the subjugation of their world by oppressive, condescending liberals. First, in the name of free trade and globalisation, they sold out their jobs and left their communities in ruin; then they told them how to think and what they could and could not say, as if they were some kind of inferior race who did not know their place or what was good for them. And a Black man and his Black wife were in the White House.

For these and other grievances, the Democrats have no answer; in part because there is no ready remedy for them, but mainly because, with Trump's relentless prodding, and much additional help from Fox News and funding from wealthy interests, the grievances have hardened into quasi-religious dogma, a psychosis, which is to say an unreality, that will not be shifted by reason or any form of relief.

The mistake might be to think that they are drawn to Trump for what he is, rather than what he represents. Better to think of him not as the enchanter of the masses, but as the embodiment of their neuroses. When we say that Trump has turned the Republican party into a cult, we forget that the cult has made Trump its own. Back in 2016 when he said, "I alone can fix it," he sounded less like Jesus on the Mount than some gilded idol with a recording inside it. That did not stop the idolising. As MAGA is his creature, Trump is theirs.

If their enthusiasm seems irrational, that is because it *is* irrational. He is not their instructor but their avatar. It doesn't matter that he talks baloney, rarely bothers to make a case, lies and has no shame; or that he talks about his own troubles, demands sympathy and never offers it. Hulk Hogan never spoke for his audience either: he didn't need to, because as Hulkamaniacs their devotion was assured. Trump said he could shoot someone on Fifth Avenue and they'd still vote for him: in truth he could vomit on them. There is no obscenity, no horror, they would not take as another sign of his incredible awesomeness. As it did in 2016, his victory will assert the meaning of *their* world, whatever needs it satisfies in his world. Losing would be their world denied, a prospect as unbearable for them as it would be for Trump's insatiable vanity.

Liberals trying to understand Trump's support might have to look more to the passions than to reason. Think of the "racist, sexist, homophobic, xenophobic, Islamophobic" views of Hillary Clinton's "basket of deplorables" as expressions of existential dismay, the survival emotions that take hold of people who feel like they've been left abandoned by the main pack and are at least subliminally living with intimations of death.

Among MAGA's antecedents at a Tea Party I attended in southeastern Ohio on 4 July 2009, there were misfits, outsiders, clueless disaffected people, manifestly lonely and aggrieved people, people whose families had been on welfare so long they'd forgotten where it came from, people with little but patriotism to hang on to: people from the "broken communities" that young J.D. Vance wrote about back in 2016 when he was telling people that Donald Trump was "cultural heroin," "the needle in America's collective vein," and warning them to beware "America's Hitler," who was leading them into "a dark place." They were the beggars outside the temple with nothing to lose, or so they became convinced. They were looking for the messiah. In 2009 they thought it might be, of all people, a woman from Alaska named Sarah Palin. They chanted, "Go, Sarah, go!" But Sarah wasn't the one.

The Tea Party people might have been guilty of some or all of the prejudices that Hillary Clinton charged them with. But it's not so long since the same attitudes would show up in a roomful of liberals. You do not have to travel far in any direction to find them now. You can find them among people who, content or fruitfully occupied in their lives, have learned to refrain from uttering them. A lot of good and generous citizens are prejudiced. But it takes a demagogue to make prejudice an ideology and the main force in their lives, and the demagogue's task is made easier when liberals sound like they are prejudiced against them.

This rendering is too soft, of course; if Trump is a danger to democracy, the MAGA folk, his footsoldiers, are also dangerous. The white supremacist, Hitler-admiring Proud Boys are resurgent. The country's far right "is as emboldened, as strong, as ready for violence as it has ever been," an academic researcher says. Two-thirds of Americans, according to polls, are worried about violence after the November election. Unlikely as it seems, the Proud Boys are not so out of step with Trump's more respectable supporters: Christian conservatives, the archetypal "normies," for instance. The Boys rose out of the same cultural moment as #MeToo. "The birth of it really was fighting this idea of toxic masculinity," one of their leaders says. They want men back in charge, women back home having babies, men not watching porn, playing video games and smoking weed, but being good fathers – with regular visits to men-only clubs where they won't feel so lonely and adrift. Add a loathing for LGBTQIA (or even just one of them), multiculturalism, Black Lives Matter, all forms of wokeism, all forms of identity politics in which the identity is not their own, liberals and a belief in the Great Replacement (or even just a suspicion that it might be true) and we have the basis of a happy marriage between Proud Boy and Oath Keepers – "Western Chauvinists" – and Christian nationalists. Other conspiracy theories, such as QAnon, are no less compatible: whither Jesus goes, Satan and his Democratic cabals of child sex traffickers and Covid-19 vaccine killers go also; along with that half of the US population reckoned to believe in demons and the preacher/exorcists who drive them out through every human orifice – cancer, ADHD, gluten intolerance, begone! – and praying for deliverance from the evil in Joe Biden and Kamala Harris. Emerging from the Age of Reason and shaped by never-ending frontiers of knowledge and invention, including the present one centred in Silicon Valley, much of the United States is as if still attached to the seventeenth century, not the eighteenth when it was born. Pizza aside, "Pizzagate" could be an episode of the Thirty Years War. In many parts the people favour the laws of God over the laws of Nature. As the Natural laws include the "natural" rights enshrined in the founding documents, these Americans are at odds with their foundations. The mistake is to think that stories as improbable as Pizzagate won't last long.

And connection to the unconnected? Maybe not. On one reading, far from connecting people, the platform on which modern conspiracy theories depend has created the solitariness of the Hobbesian state of nature. We have Silicon Valley to thank for engineering a much more atomised, lonelier society than the one lamented by philosophers, notably Hannah Arendt, and political scientists such as Robert Putnam, last century. It was loneliness, Arendt said, that "prepared men for totalitarian domination." Putnam, in *Bowling Alone*, argued that declining social interaction, caused in large part by television and the internet, had undermined the civic engagement that democracy relies on – and Tocqueville noted 190 years ago. If joining a church – or trade union, sorority or Lions Club – offers an answer to loneliness, signing up to a conspiracy theory provides a more complete one, because the technology on which it depends is self-sustaining, being at once a symptom, a cause and a solution for the solitary individual. Like many churches, a conspiracy theory is easy to join, much harder to leave. QAnon has gone quiet since the 6 January 2021 insurrection, where it was prominently represented, but millions of Americans retain the faith, and no one knows how many children have been infected.

The Great Replacement is the (conspiracy) theory, first made popular on the internet by Renaud Camus, that an international elite is set on replacing the established white population and cultures of Europe with cheap and politically biddable migrants from the Global South. In the US the fear reflects the fact that white people who were 80 per cent of the population in the

1950s are now 58 per cent, and the day is coming when they will no longer be the majority. In Tucker Carlson's definition, the elites (liberals, Democrats, Joe Biden, Kamala Harris, George Soros, "They") are deliberately encouraging the replacement of "legacy Americans with more obedient people from faraway countries." "Legacy Americans" are not Cherokees or Algonquians or people like that: they are Americans genetically or culturally descended, allowing for some inevitable modifications, from the white people who were in a majority at the time of the nation's founding – or something of that kind. "Faraway countries" are not Australia or New Zealand, but geographically adjacent Central and South American countries, most of which are closer to Washington, DC, than Seattle and San Francisco are.

There are legacy Americans (also known as white people), and there are the people (also known as Black people or people of colour) Donald Trump calls "vermin" – "rapists," "murderers," "animals" – who are replacing them, or rather "poisoning the blood" of the United States. A University of Massachusetts Amherst poll found that 35 per cent of Trump's 2020 voters also thought these people were "poisoning the blood" of the country, two-thirds thought they threatened American "culture and identity" and 76 per cent agreed with the theory of "obedient voters." According to the poll, 43 per cent of Americans, including 24 per cent of Democrats and 41 per cent of independents, accept the Replacement theory as fact. Elon Musk, who is backing Trump, also backs the theory.

A believer in the Great Replacement killed twenty-one Latinos in El Paso, another killed eleven Jews in a Pittsburgh synagogue, and another killed ten African Americans in Buffalo. Great Replacement theorists with Nazi and confederate flags yelled, "You will not replace us" and "Jews will not replace us" in Charlottesville, before one of them drove his car into a crowd of nonbelievers. Many among the January 6 mob at the Capitol believed in the Great Replacement. Trump has fed the theory for eight years and he feeds it every day when he talks about the "invasion" of the United States by illegal immigrants. The political scientist Jesse Rhodes says there is a "significant market" for authoritarianism in the United States. This we know to be true because, leaving aside the original conquest, the first Replacement theory took possession of the American mind in the days of slavery and has never released its grip.

If he knows nothing else, Trump knows it is essential to be interesting. He's not the first influential American to deal fiction as fact. The advertising agencies have been in that game for years. Almost as long as Hollywood. What is the Dream without a bit of make-believe? Trump's most distinguished predecessor might be Silas Ratcliffe of Henry Adams' *Democracy*, published in 1880. From the Midwest frontier rather than Queens, and a more articulate reptile by far, Ratcliffe is nevertheless, like Trump, an outsider determined to push aside the well-born elites he despises and make Washington his own. He's a whatever-it-takes politician: a narcissist, an iconoclast, a user, a supreme pragmatist; Mrs Lee, the woman he insists must be his wife, calls him a "moral lunatic."

Capable spin doctors could not fail to recognise something of their craft in Ratcliffe's fervent rationalisations. Asked what can be done about corruption (in which he is himself engaged), he replies that no representative government can be much better than the society it represents. "Purify society and you purify the government. But try to purify the government artificially and you only aggravate failure." No one knows this better than Trump. He knows that society can't be purified, if only because Donald Trump is part of it. But he's a purifier nonetheless: he'll get rid of the immigrants corrupting it, "the communists, Marxists, fascists, and the radical left thugs that live like vermin within the confines of our country," the liberals ruining it, the swamp feeding off it, the foreign countries taking it for a ride. Purifying society is half his schtick, and the other half is purifying the government by making it, in essence, him. That's what makes Trump an enemy of democracy, or if you prefer, an instrument of American fascism.

Eight years ago, mainstream liberal Democrats were not willing to call Trump what he was. They called him a populist, specifically a "right-wing populist," which distinguished him from the "left-wing populist" Bernie Sanders. In both cases the word was a distraction: from Sanders' social democratic policies and from the ideology that informed Trump's demagoguery. The success of both "populists" showed up the failings of both major parties, the disconnect between mainstream politics and the reality of life for millions. Trump the populist won the election. There is plenty to indicate that the populist Sanders would have succeeded where Hillary Clinton failed.

In the 2016 election Trump's opponents called him a bully, a misogynist, a liar, a serial groper, a malignant narcissist, a tax cheat, a fraudster. They used terms that went to his character, almost as if his manners, rather than his politics and his world view, were the worst things about him. It was not hard to see why. He *was* loathsome. His lies were so frequent and so outrageous, how could any reasonable person, which liberals tend to assume they are, not be outraged? His behaviour was so objectionable, how could they not object? He was so ridiculous, how could they not mock? They went after him on these grounds because in those long-ago days it was generally assumed that no candidate could survive so many proven charges, or even such swaggering vulgarity.

But for Trump, their rage was gold: more proof that his opponents were the fools he said they were. Let them call him a gangster. Gangsters are a staple of the American imagination. There is no America without gangsters. What sort of democracy would it be if no one had the spunk to go against the grain? What sort of America? When Hillary Clinton said she "didn't like Mr Trump's tone," Trump feasted on it. Tone! When "we have people – Christians – having their heads cut off in the Middle East," and she cares about tone! His people didn't care about tone! But Trump cares about it. He makes havoc with it.

Everyone saw the mass rallies and the strutting, pouting histrionics; the scapegoating of migrants, the xenophobia and barely disguised racism; his appeals to a mythic past; his cultivation of popular fantasies of grievance, betrayal, plots and conspiracies; his self-portrayal as the great leader who alone could rid Americans – real Americans – of the oppressive elites; the anti-intellectualism; the bullying regard for strength, and loathing for weakness; and of course the endless lies. Some commentators used the word "autocratic." Some said "authoritarian." Very few were prepared to say "fascist." Michael Moore did, the same Michael Moore who said Trump would win if Hillary Clinton was the candidate, but no respectable liberal was going to line up with the hairy shit-stirrer – even if he made sense. It is true that the left has often misused the word, but that does not mean fascism is dead and buried, or that democracies are immune to its appeal. Umberto Eco called it Ur-Fascism or "eternal fascism." In 1995 he wrote, "Ur-Fascism can come back under the most innocent of disguises. Our duty is to uncover it and point the finger at any of its new instances – every day and in every part of the world." In 2016 the commentators and Trump's opponents refrained from pointing the finger.

This year it's different. The words "autocracy," "dictator" and "authoritarian" – and, yes, "fascist" – now turn up everywhere, including in the columns of stalwart *New York Times* contributors. Thomas Friedman prefers to call the Republican party a cult, and Trump therefore a cult leader, and but one short step from a dictator. The cover of *The Economist* on 16 May 2024 was headlined "Is America Dictator Proof?" The lead article was typically cautious but reported the disturbing fact that one in four Americans thought autocracy a good idea, even a "very good" one. The cover of *The New Republic*, left-leaning admittedly but not that far, had Trump with a Hitler moustache. In *The Atlantic* Tom Nichols shed his reluctance to use the word, but stressed caution because many supporters of Trump were not fascists. The same of course could be said about many supporters of Hitler and Mussolini. We could say it's not worth arguing over labels, or we could say that because Trumpism lacks the military dimension of German and Italian fascism it is not fascist. Perhaps Trump is just an errant monomaniac, or even a man constructing a self-parodying "Donald the Fascist" wrestling persona. But history's fascists have often presented as clowns and gormless misfits. To imagine what is possible in the next four years, or the next three months, we need only take ourselves back to the beginning of 2015: no one, not even Trump by some accounts, thought he could be president. Now the man twice impeached, facing a host of criminal charges, a fraudster, a liar and a crook, is in the race to be president again.

Anything could happen. The billionaire founder of the country's biggest hedge fund reckons there's a one in three chance of civil war. More than half of all Republican voters say they expect civil war. The most popular movie in April was *Civil War*. A Supreme Court justice flies the US flag upside down outside his house in a signal of his support for the 6 January 2021 "insurrection" and Trump's refusal to accept the result of the 2020 election. Trump tells an audience in Minnesota that they have "good genes." He is deliberately entering fascist territory, and it is surely stupid to ignore the signs he's sending.

Sceptical conservatives looking for a way out of Trump can get an alternative view and, it is fair to say, a lot more facts on the liberal news channel MSNBC. But they may not find enchantment. MSNBC is not loud and sometimes deranged like Fox, but after a while you pick up the beats. A revelation a decade ago, it is now a liberal church, pleasing no doubt to the converted, but unlikely to persuade an uncommitted viewer that they are not the pious pains in the arse the right says they are. At first, it's not so much the hymns as the way they sing them; and after an hour or two of that, it's the hymns. The crew lack self-awareness. Nothing would so decisively set the channel apart from Fox – and way above it – as Rachel Maddow laughing at herself, or *Morning Joe* getting a dose of Philip Marlowe's drollery. Failing anything so radical, they could do worse than get out Robert Kennedy's speech in Indianapolis a couple of hours after Martin Luther King was killed (and eight weeks before Kennedy was) and put it on repeat. Not to imitate Kennedy – heaven help us if they try – or to get a modern audience to heed the words of Aeschylus that he quoted, but to be reminded that tone can be as persuasive as substance, that substance without the right tone is worse than useless and that for practical purposes the two are the same thing.

On a huge billboard in the provinces, passing motorists can see the words of the Old Testament prophet Isaiah: "Unto us a son is given and the government shall be upon his shoulders." Beside the words, a photo of

Donald Trump, digitally doctored to make him all-wise and benign. And beneath Trump the words "Joint Heirs: Romans 8:17," wherein Paul says we are the children of God, and "if children, then heirs: heirs of God, and joint heirs with Christ; if so be that we suffer with him, that we may be also glorified together." The surrounding passages of the New Testament concern hope and deliverance from the "sufferings of this present time."

Christianity offers solace, but from Christianity-plus-Trump glory beckons. He feeds them hope and glory, they offer him charisma. This is how armies are made.

Of course, Hollywood did other types as well: out-of-towners both innocent and sinister, fresh-faced gals and guys, Goofy, Scrooge McDuck, conspirators, gunslingers, preachers, God-fearing farmers, cowboys and Indians, bumpkins, hulks, spidermen and spiderwomen, not to mention countless portrayals of real historical figures. Day after day they still churn it out – content. Hollywood has created a comprehensive shadow world of human types and human predicaments, half imaginary and half representative, and they have sent it around the world. This is why, for an outsider, the place resembles a theme park; it would be unbelievable if it were not so familiar. Buster Keaton was onto it in 1924: in *Sherlock Jr.* he took his romantic cues from the film he was projecting and walked through the screen and into the action. Americans have been living in these intersecting worlds ever since. The wonder is most of them seem sane.

Both sides of politics think the entertainment industry is crucial to their chances. The Democrats have Beyoncé in their camp, and pray that Taylor Swift will step up for them, as she has in the past – and with measurable effect on the number of young people registering to vote. Trump has a problem with Swift. Surveys have found that somewhere between a quarter and a half of Americans are "Swifties." Put aside a vain old man's fantasies, Trump does not want to offend such a powerful woman. Deep down he surely knows she won't come his way, but perhaps he can persuade her to stay neutral. If only he had words to praise her that did not make him sound like a creep. He says she's "beautiful – very beautiful" and "unusually beautiful." In a single post he used the word "beautiful" five times but couldn't come up with anything about her talent, her songs or her acumen. He can't be the only one who gets all tongue-tied when he thinks about her, but her other fans don't claim to be "more popular" than she is, as Trump does, or threaten "holy war" against her if she swings behind Biden.

Biden had Steven Spielberg on board, and Kamala Harris has Barbra Streisand, and the Democrats have the great majority of celebrity performers. In a discombobulating appearance outside the Manhattan courthouse where Trump was being tried, Robert de Niro shouted at the former president's supporters that their man was a "gangster." Apart from being a bit like a virtual pot calling a kettle black, the moment left sensible people wondering why Biden needed a method actor to perform his lines for him.

Jeffrey Katzenberg, the hyper-energetic movie mogul who co-founded DreamWorks and produced *The Lion King* and *Shrek*, among hundreds of other films, threw a fundraiser for the Democrats in March. He got Stephen Colbert and presidents Clinton and Obama along and raised $26 million. Katzenberg is a long-time Democrat supporter. He had the ear of Obama, but for Biden he had much more. He was co-chair of his campaign committee and a regular in the West Wing, and primed the president for his surprisingly forceful State of the Union address in early 2024. Katzenberg is said to be driven by hearing from his European-born grandparents that in the 1930s they did not believe Hitler was a real threat. He brings that sort of personal conviction with everything he knows about stories and how to tell them. He cast Biden as Mufasa, the wise old lion of *The Lion King*. Trump, inevitably, is Scar, the villain who kills him.

In LA on 15 June, Katzenberg put together another Biden fundraiser with George Clooney, Julia Roberts, Barbara Streisand, Jimmy Kimmel and a host of very rich Los Angelenos. Obama was there again, along with Gavin Newsom, the governor of California (who has presidential ambitions), and the mayor of LA, Karen Bass (who might also have ambitions – so many people do). Top price for a ticket was half a million dollars, which got you a photograph with Barack, George, Julia and Joe, access through a VIP entrance and an invitation to the after-party.

Clooney, it cannot be denied, is every bit the "elitist Hollywood celebrity," as the Trump camp calls such supporters, but these days he's a bit more than that. He recently complained to the White House about Biden announcing the US was considering sanctions against the International Criminal Court and describing as "outrageous" the court's decision to issue arrest warrants for Benjamin Netanyahu. The US does not recognise the ICC. Clooney does, of course; his wife, Amal, has more than once appeared before the court on behalf of victims of war crimes, and she worked on the case against Netanyahu. But neither party was so petty as to allow the contretemps to spoil the harmony of the evening, which raised more than $30 million.

Could any amount of money save Mufasa? How many celebrity endorsements are needed to save the old lion from going the way he went in the film? Then again, it seems possible, even likely, that every spectacle of the liberal elites drives away as many voters as it attracts. The telling moment came at the end, although at the time it went unreported. As the band played exit music and the stars were leaving the stage, the president "appeared to freeze," and only unfroze when Obama went to his side and with a hand on his arm guided him away. Someone took a picture, and the picture told a story that seemed increasingly likely to end with the demise of Joe Biden.

*

The Santa Monica Freeway, as wide as the Missouri but flowing ten times faster, is an LA artery: in the body of the nation, it's a capillary. You half drive these freeways and are half carried like flotsam, racketing along until you shoot off up a ramp and find yourself in another America. It's not unlike an election.

In 1933 the crime fiction writer James M. Cain admired the roads of Los Angeles, many of which even then were eight lanes wide: "superb," he said. What impressed him less were the signs on either side of them. The Spanish chapter in Californian history was closed; the new one was nothing but "an endless succession of Rabbit Fryers, 50c; Eggs, Guaranteed Fresh, 23c a Doz.; Canary Birds, 50c, Also Baby Chix, Just Hatched; Car Mart, All Makes Used Cars … Drink Goat Milk for Health …" and so on. The streets and strip malls of the United States maintain that tradition, but with fewer rabbit fryers and canaries and more fried chicken and nail salons, hair salons, holistic health salons, tanning salons and Brazilian wax salons.

The charmless aesthetic of roadside commerce was bad enough, but what really concerned Cain were the "piddling" fly-by-night occupations into which the economy of the place had consigned the vendors of goat milk and orange peelers, and the incompetence of everyone from waiters to movie impresarios who, until the sunny skies of California lured them west, had been herding swine in Iowa or mending skirts in Brooklyn. No one was the person they had been a year or two before, or the person they hoped to be a year or two hence. Little wonder "nutty religions" were multiplying; people were desperate to find a point to their lives.

The problem was the lack of substantial industry: oil, movies and funerals were not enough to run on. Cain reckoned LA needed industries that bound people together, that produced competence, pride and "pep." Such industries, he surmised, might also dissipate the anti-labour feeling that everyone in town seemed to share.

Today the long, wide street that takes you to Koreatown is lined with the usual salons, and the usual fried chicken, acupuncturists, realtors and vape suppliers, along with vendors of tofu and tasty Korean barbecue. Except for a few grand survivors of the art deco era, such as the Pellissier Building and the Wiltern Theatre, the streetscape is unattractive without being downright ugly. But it does not look poor. Race riots in 1992 might have meant the end of Koreatown, but the place revived and, despite a recent surge in (mainly anti-Asian, Covid-related) hate crimes, it now thrives.

Bernie arrived in the US from the Philippines twenty-seven years ago. He's spent the last twenty-four years in Los Angeles. He remains an undocumented migrant, one of at least 10.5 million in the United States. He has no green card, no US passport, which means should he leave the country he'd never get back in. He lives in a rented apartment in Koreatown with his second wife, a Filipina, and their twenty-year-old son. Being undocumented does not mean he can't get a driver's licence, or buy health insurance, rent a flat or get Covid jabs. After many years of trying, he hopes to have US citizenship next year. He'd like to visit his children in the Philippines and Australia, but LA is where he wants to live.

Four days a week, he works for Amazon; sometimes in the warehouse, the rest of the time driving all over LA, delivering and picking up "mainly books and vitamins." On other days he works as a carer. We met in a sort of Filipino-French café that sold coffee and pastries. Bernie likes Koreatown well enough: it's safe if you stay with the Asian people, he says, and keep away from the Black areas. He says this with no apparent spite, as if it were simply a bit of the physical environment to avoid. His apartment has rent control, but elsewhere rents – and prices – are too high. Life is harder than it used to be. Downtown is bad. Many homeless people are living on the street there, he says. He sees their camps when his job takes him there.

Over three days every January, about 6000 volunteers spread out across the metropolis to count the homeless people. Last year they found 75,518 in the county and 46,260 in the city. That is 70 to 80 per cent more than there were in 2015, 12 per cent more than since the pandemic. There are four times more Black people than white among the homeless. Low wages, high rents and a lack of affordable housing swell the number, even though the city has placed more than 21,000 in leased hotels. Drug addiction swells it further. Fentanyl, an opioid 50 to 100 times stronger than morphine, is the main killer. In 2022, across the United States more than 107,000 people died from opioid and methamphetamine overdoses, 30,000 deaths involved cocaine and another 10,000 from drugs described as "natural/semi-synthetic." One in every three homeless adults in LA is a fentanyl or methamphetamine addict. On average, six die every day.

California is the worst state for homelessness. Among cities, Los Angeles runs a close second to New York. Seattle, Portland, Denver, San Diego and Boston – all run by Democrats – are not far behind. Donald Trump points to these places as examples of liberal incompetence and failure, and proof of the Democrats' responsibility for America's decay. He calls Gavin Newsom, the telegenic governor of California and presidential aspirant, Gavin "New Scum." He is "bullshit," he says. His government is "unbelievable" and "horrible."

Bernie takes no interest in politics, or at least affects none, and is not concerned by Trump's threat to throw out undocumented people: he shrugs and smiles, which might signify the fatalism of the powerless, the fringe dweller, the person without horizons; or it might mean that Bernie knows they can't deport the people on whom the quality of American life substantially depends. Who will drive the Ubers, deliver the meals, care for the children and the aged, milk the cows, pick the fruit, walk the dogs, clean the toilets, man the leaf blowers? Bernie's son, who is finishing a degree, intends to escape those fates. He is interested in politics and leans Democrat.

Bernie said he would drive me back to where I was staying. I assumed it would be in one of the ageing Hondas and Toyotas in the car park. But it was the late-model BMW we went to. "Nice car," I said. "Amazon," he said with a smile. He wound his way expertly through the traffic, through Beverly and some of the more expensive real estate on Earth, through the hordes of giant black SUVs beloved of government officials, FBI agents and conscientious moms. He knew where I was going because his job often took him there. Forty minutes later, when we turned off Sunset Boulevard, he said, "Nice here. Lot of money." "You sell a lot of vitamins here?" I asked. "Yes," he said, "lot of vitamins."

*

The driver who took me to Los Angeles airport told me that he had once owned a successful construction company. It is not uncommon in that line of work. He'd had six trucks, seven tractors and fifteen employees. His Filipina wife was long gone, but he had never wanted for female company, and only some of them had he paid for (*laughter*), and none of them had demanded as much as Stormy Daniels (*laughter*). We passed the Shangri La hotel in Santa Monica, where, it is said, Bill Clinton often had female company (*laughter*).

The big man next to me on the plane, whose leg and elbow occupied 15 per cent of the part of the aircraft for which I had paid, played a video game on his laptop without a break for four hours. I could see the screen: a soldier, a mercenary of some kind, running, dodging machine-gun fire and grenades, his tireless, hypnotic gait carrying him through jungle, menacing streets and bombed-out ruins. Killing the enemy as he ran. The soldier was still running, and the passenger was still engrossed, when the plane bumped onto the tarmac.

Happy Indian music boomed from Harvinder's radio, and Harvinder was happy too. He loved the United States, especially Ann Arbor, his chosen home. In America "you choose your lifestyle," he told me. After trying New York and Los Angeles he chose Michigan because it was "so green and quiet" and he was free to "go wherever" he liked. It was not what he said but the manner of his saying it, the pleasure he took in the world he had found. A few months earlier he had been granted citizenship. It was just a matter of filling in the paperwork. Without the paperwork you are "shit." He had filled it in, again and again and again, for twelve years. Then the day came – they said yes. Heaven!

I never met a happier man than Harvinder. We talked about cricket, of course. He had a special aerial on his house so he could watch every match. But he liked American sports as well. I sidestepped Narendra Modi and went straight to Trump. "I will vote for him," he said. "They are both bad candidates, but it should be Trump. You know why?" I didn't. "Because every day, every morning, I turn on my phone and he's said something, some word, just a word." He laughed. Trump ignited his days. "*Every* day he does. I love it." He laughed louder.

That day, in an interview published in *The New York Times*, Hillary Clinton blamed former FBI director James Comey for her loss in 2016, which in the long run has cost American women their reproductive rights. In July that year, Comey said that as secretary of state Clinton had been "extremely careless" in her handling of emails. That was bad enough. Then a few days before the election he announced the FBI was reopening its investigation into the matter. He has recently given his reasons and expressed his hope that the FBI did not inadvertently bring about Clinton's defeat. Voters held her to account, she says, because as a woman she is expected to be perfect, whereas Trump, being a man, was forgiven his "flaws."

That seemed a fair analysis. But in these early days of an election that Clinton and many others are calling "existential," it also seemed impolitic.

It was not that she was dodging responsibility for losing, and by losing opening the way for a Supreme Court that overturned *Roe v. Wade*. It was that griping, however understandable, darkens the political mood. Clinton has grown close to Kamala Harris, and no doubt provides the vice president with invaluable tactical and moral support. Given the agony of her defeat in 2016 and the fact that Harris campaigned against her and for Obama in the 2008 primaries, Clinton's sisterly embrace is almost saintly. The long experience of a woman in a male-dominated domain, and the example of her courage and resilience, can only help the VP. Maybe Harris has also taken something from less positive examples: keep smiling, but not so much that the 5 per cent of voters you need in Pennsylvania and the northern Midwest don't think you're the epitome of the smug meritocrat who doesn't get it. And don't just talk, go there and take an industry policy with you. Blame Harvinder's cheerfulness in Michigan's spring sunshine, but the recital of Clinton's grievances sounded indulgent, even if it also sounded in tune with MSNBC. Of course, the Democrats' hostility to Trump and their stress on the threat he poses is justified: *so* justified that if they gave it a rest for a fortnight and concentrated on the cost of living, it would still be justified when they took it up again.

The autocrat offers to take care of things. He needn't say how, only that he will do what his followers want done, what is necessary, what is just. His followers give themselves up to his promise. He'll take care of their needs and (in the other meaning of the term) take care of their enemies: the freeloaders who take real Americans for mugs; the liberal elites who take them for granted; the immigrants who are taking their jobs, their hotel rooms, their safety, even their lives. Their country. The autocrat who derides identity politics practises it in an extreme form.

The stories that Americans have told themselves are stories of becoming: becoming a republic, a democracy, the most powerful nation on earth. What is true of the nation is true of the individual: the immigrant becomes an American, the American becomes a millionaire, a star, the dream made real. MAGA complains that America can't "become" because it is bogged down in wars and clogged up with taxes and regulations. Americans can no longer live the American dream, can't *have* the dream. Immigrants are dreaming it instead.

The Democrats are stuck with the traditional form of the story: new frontiers unfolding, a future full of promise, a more just society, a more perfect union … the vision thing. The story is fine but early in June there were two obstacles to telling it. The first was Joe Biden, who did not lack hope and vision but represented the past and often looked becalmed. The second was Trump. The man's lies are so frequent, his behaviour so obnoxious and his positions so offensive, he demands rebuttal every day. But by incessantly belting away at Trump, the Democrats run the risk of forfeiting a story of their own.

It is essential to both Trump's WrestleMania persona and his strategy to be assailed by outraged liberals. Nothing makes Donald Trump and his cohorts happier than what Fox News calls "Trump derangement syndrome." To save democracy, Democrats must deny them that pleasure. They need to glow a little with democracy's liberating virtues, reason, hope and happiness among them. They must point towards happiness, as the Declaration recommended; or towards material security and wellbeing, which is what most people hope for and wish governments would provide. This much Trump understands, and the more he understands it, the more the Democrats waste their energy crying "felon," "liar," "dictator." They could do worse than imitate the example of Bernie Sanders, who rarely gives the man more than a single contemptuous sentence before taking up his unwavering themes. But once the Democrats allow themselves to be defined by their opposition to Trump, the fight is as good as lost.

*

Like the great majority of US hotels, this one was miles from downtown Ann Arbor, and surrounded by roads, car parks and other chain hotels, all serving the same breakfast and testifying to the same general conviction that a car and a person are one indivisible unit. The young woman at the hotel must have been watching *Schitt's Creek*. When I asked her if any of the rooms had a view, she said, "A view of what? A dumpster or a gas station?" I said, "Don't you have one with a tree?" She scanned the screen and after a moment said with a smile, "Oh yes, we do – there's a tree next to the dumpster."

"If you want to know about a culture, spend a night in its bars," Hemingway said. These days you can learn as much from its car parks. Still, he had a point, even if he was rationalising his addiction, as he was when he said he drank "to make other people seem interesting." The bar had a view of two TV sets on different channels. I remember the first time I sat on a stool in an American bar and in that moment felt I had joined with the country. There is nothing mean about an American bar. No measuring the whisky in those miserable little measuring jiggers, they just poured it straight from the bottle to the glass. They did not ask you to pay for each drink, you paid when you left. They did not ask you how your day had been so far – nothing so crass and intrusive – but what they could do for me, pal, or even "sir." They respected your privacy, because a public bar is also a private refuge. The American bar is where the individual finds community without being obliged to commune. The paragons of the bartending profession tend to the soul – the melancholy, the needful, the lovesick and the riotous – with kindly but disinterested poise. In *My Darling Clementine*, a wistful Wyatt Earp (Henry Fonda) says to the bartender: "Mac [*beat*], have you ever been in love?" The bartender, after a moment's reflection, says: "No. [*beat*] I've been a bartender all my life." You tip a bartender as you might a priest – for solace, but do not expect absolution.

The woman on the adjacent stool was staring not into her drink, but at her laptop, setting up tomorrow's program. The man at the far end was poking around in a salad, drinking a microbrewery beer and occasionally fixing on one of the TVs where CBS News was running without the sound on. On the other screen it was softball, with the sound: Oklahoma playing Florida. A blonde Brunnhilde pitching to a diminutive Black woman. The stands were packed. The young softballers – Black women, white women, brown women – muscular and bursting with health and white teeth, were playing and emoting all over the place, as if a game of softball was the nearest thing to ecstasy or full-blown war. In the bar, no one noticed. The barman had it differently to Hemingway. Seeing me writing notes, he said, "I'm a writer too, but working in this bar I don't find people interesting anymore."

"The prevailing social conditions not only encourage a defensive contraction of the self, but blur the boundaries between the self and its surroundings." The social critic Christopher Lasch wrote that forty years ago. There had been a social transformation, he said: "the replacement of a reliable world of durable objects by a world of flickering images that make it harder to distinguish reality from fantasy." In this chain hotel far beyond the heartbeat of the city, it did seem that the bartender was all that stood between the patrons and total immersion in the flickering images. They had long ago become willing citizens of the atomised, disaggregated culture of the automobile and the town planners. If the bonds of common interest had withered in that environment, the more appealing the screens of the social media community were bound to be.

In the middle of the night an ear-splitting alarm went off and the hotel's guests trotted out into the car park. A fire in the laundry had filled the halls with smoke. Two pulsating, blaring fire trucks roared up. Then a third. The firemen strode in. Each man had attached to his body enough equipment to deal with any imaginable situation, including, I thought for some reason, aliens. Probably it was the star-filled sky we were standing under in our pyjamas, but it was also those firefighters' chiselled jaws, bulging chests and ballooning biceps. I have never seen such upper bodies, except in American comics and TV cartoons about firemen.

In Ann Arbor the creamy white dogwoods were out. The cafés and bookshops were thronged. In the open-air market, ageing boomers sold the stuff they've been selling in such markets for half a century. A billboard acknowledged that the land they were selling it on "was the ancestral, traditional, and contemporary homeland of many indigenous nations" and that "most, if not all, of the land of this nation was obtained in unconscionable ways." A "painful history of genocide and forced relocation," the sign said. What it said is true, beyond doubt; and it is also true that, faced with the same resistance to its ambitions, the nation would do it all over again. Nothing is unconscionable – it's just a word. Ann Arbor, built around the 700-acre campus of the highly ranked and splendidly endowed University of Michigan, is a liberal city, a Democrat city. It is also a white city: 70 per cent white, about 12 per cent Black. In Detroit, forty miles away, those figures are reversed.

DETROIT

> *There are cities that get by on their good looks, offer climate and scenery, views of mountains or oceans, rockbound or with palm trees; and there are cities like Detroit that have to work for a living.*
>
> Elmore Leonard

> *Every fourteen seconds Wierzbicki reams a bearing and Stephanides grinds a bearing and O'Mally attaches a bearing to a camshaft.*
>
> Jeffrey Eugenides, *Middlesex*

"If you want to know about America, study Detroit," they say. That's true enough. The glowing CBD, the pleasant suburbs, the fine old institutions and the new industries fired by new technology – America the good. The crime, corruption, poverty and addiction, the race and class divide, the derelict suburbs – America the bad. A fallen city. Yet the furious belief that the city will revive, will be born again, that God will be in the whirlwind – America the eternally hopeful.

The Uber driver hated his Tesla Model Y, the world's best-selling car. He thought it was "crap." He could not separate the car from the company that made it, or the company from its founder. He hated Elon Musk and the rest of the billionaire class. He hated the private equity firms that bought the retail stores Sears and Hudson's and Crowley's, "places that meant a lot to people," and stripped them out and sold the real estate. "Rich folks only care about their money," he said. "So they move their plants to Mexico or somewhere and leave places like Detroit and Flint and Lansing to decay. The only patriots are the poor people." He was driving up Woodward Avenue, the city's broad backbone that ends in the phalanx of skyscrapers on the waterfront. The Detroit Institute of Arts and Wayne State are on Woodward. The big events happen on this street. In Elmore Leonard's novels, criminals and their pursuers are always going up and down and across Woodward. The Uber driver hated Trump too. He worried about what he might do. "As a Black man," he said, "I am frightened."

In the first half of the twentieth century, white folk from the economically depressed regions of the United States, especially Appalachia and the South; Black folk from the South and east-coast cities where wages were low and jobs hard for Blacks to get; Poles, Greeks, Irish, Italians, Germans, and people from the Middle East and the countries of Central America were all drawn to Detroit by the unstoppable car industry and the promise of five dollars a day. Now a little over half a million people live in a city which in 1960 was home to 1.8 million, the fourth-biggest city in the United States. And 82 per cent of the population is now Black.

Detroit was not just any city: Detroit was Motor City, the *American* city of wide and leafy streets, suburbs of detached single-family bungalows, and a waterfront downtown of glamorous art deco and Beaux-Arts towers looking across the river to modest Canada. It was the city of Ford, General Motors and Chrysler, and the advertising industry that made their cars universal objects of desire; the city of thousands of workers, protected by powerful unions, going to and from the factories clutching their lunch pails. Detroit is where Henry Ford came up with the Model T and the assembly line on which about 5000 parts were put together to make a car in just 93 minutes, so efficiently and cheaply that Ford could sell them for less than $500 and, with the reasonable wages paid them, workers could afford to buy one – though rarely Black workers, who were invariably employed in more gruelling and poorly paid roles in the foundries or as janitors.

Detroit gave America millions of T-Model and A-Model Fords. It gave the world the methods of mass industrial production known as Fordism by which the cars were made. Fordism owed something to the scientific management theories of Frederick Winslow Taylor, something to the disassembling of cattle on the meat-processing chains of Chicago slaughterhouses, and something to the ruthless genius of Henry Ford. The assembly line did more than produce goods efficiently: it changed common human experience, the relationship between human beings and machines; between the mind and the body, Jean-Paul Sartre said, and Charlie Chaplin demonstrated it on film.

Fordism was more than the assembly line. Inspectors from Ford's "Sociological Department" routinely visited employees' home to make sure they were meeting company standards of cleanliness and sobriety and living the "American lifestyle," which was to say the essentially petit-bourgeois ideal of "normal" nuclear families and regular churchgoing. Henry Ford believed in a melting pot of cultures from which standardised Americans would emerge like his standardised cars.

In pursuit of this ideal, in the '30s he offered something like a corporate alternative to Roosevelt's New Deal – which he hated. He provided low-cost food, low-interest loans for houses and home improvements, and he built schools. The Italian Marxist Antonio Gramsci wrote that the dependence created by these measures fostered in turn the discipline and compliance workers needed to withstand the pressures of sped-up production lines, and that capitalism needed to thrive. The process by which the capitalist ruling class gained the "consent" of labour, and society more broadly, he called hegemony. Forty years later the "invisible power" that ruled minds and bodies became a central concept among New Left theorists, and in fragments, a trope of spaced-out hippies.

"Historical fact: people stopped being human in 1913," Jeffrey Eugenides said in his novel set in Detroit, *Middlesex*. Fordism was taken up in all the advanced capitalist countries, and by Joseph Stalin. Stalin admired the "indomitable efficiency" of the American industrial system. He had no Marxist or any other kind of misgivings about subjecting workers to stupefying repetition, reducing them to cogs in a machine or alienating them from the product of their labour – albeit, in the US at least, with the prospect of buying it on hire purchase. Ford built a plant for Stalin in Gorki (Nizhny Novgorod). Fascist Italy and Nazi Germany also studied and adopted Fordism, and Hitler took further inspiration from Henry Ford's antisemitic propaganda. Detroit was also home to the country's other leading antisemite, the Catholic priest Charles Edward Coughlin, "Father Coughlin," whose anti-capitalist, anti-communist, anti-Black, pro-fascist radio programs reached upwards of 30 million Americans, a quarter of the population. Naturally, the fascist governments of Italy and Japan, which, like the Nazis, sent emissaries to Detroit to learn from Ford's methods, were not put off by the company's violent repression of unionists, the system of spies and thugs it employed, and its nasty puritan snooping on the private lives of employees.

Ford's assembly line was famously memorialised by Diego Rivera's colossal murals in the Detroit Institute of Arts. That Henry Ford's only child, Edsel, should have commissioned a Mexican communist is surprising enough. The strange twist is that he did it in 1932, the year that Ford's 3000-strong machine-gun toting Security Department shot dead five striking workers and injured a couple of hundred others at the River Rouge plant.

But nothing that happens in the United States is *ever* truly surprising. In the incessant swell of cliché-riddled patriotism and dutiful observance of social rituals, its peasant-like provincialism and maudlin religiosity, it is easy to forget that America's sharpest critics have generally been American, and that the visionary, the iconoclast and the rebel are prized constituents of the culture. And sons turn against fathers sometimes. Edsel Ford was a bit of an aesthete. He changed the shape of his father's cars. And he liked art. In the 1930s, he was president of both the Ford Motor Company and the Detroit Arts Commission. He commissioned Rivera and took him to Ford's famous Albert Kahn–designed Rouge plant – a complete production system operating in ninety-three buildings on 2000 acres. The artist saw the forges and steel mills, the coke ovens, the glass factories, and the railways and the ships that crossed the lake with the raw materials to feed them; the foundries where, in smoke and steam, men – mainly Black men – converted the iron into engine blocks and cylinder heads, and thousands of other men on the assembly line performed their allotted tasks in the few seconds apportioned them: tasks so simple, Henry Ford declared, a worker needed to be "no smarter than an ox."

The cars rolled off the line and out into the world, where Americans drove them into the sunlit American future. At least the advertising agencies portrayed it that way. This was modernity. This was the United States.

On four walls of a great hall at the Institute of Arts Rivera painted murals honouring the technology and the multiracial workers, and even the besuited boater-wearing managers and time-and-motion men, the technocrats. He captured the immense scale and complexity of the operation, all of it, and much more. He painted the car plant as the seething heart of industrial capitalism, a sort of supervised bedlam with its roots in history, and with branches reaching into lives in the furthest corners of the globe. The car plant was the epitome of modern capitalism, the car – stately, gleaming freedom machine and most desired thing – was not only the engine of the economy, the shaper of worlds and mighty creator of wealth, but the indispensable component of consumerism, capitalism's core ideology. Good Marxist that he was, Rivera saw the contradictions and tempered admiration with foreboding, reverence with satire.

Pre-war, Detroit was in the vanguard of America's burgeoning global pre-eminence. During the war, when the United States became the self-styled "arsenal of democracy," the car companies of Detroit flew the flag with gusto, manufacturing prodigious amounts of military equipment, from tanks and planes to artillery and ammunition. One Ford plant turned out a B-24 bomber every hour. Once the war was over, the combination of new models and smart advertising made Detroit not just an industrial engine room but a smart, desirable, *essential* American city.

When Henry Ford II (grandson of the original and known as "The Deuce") took over the company in 1945, he set out to repair relations with Jewish Americans. He began in Hollywood, where the damage was illustrated by Harry Warner, who had forbidden any employee of Warner Brothers, including Gary Cooper, to drive a Ford on the company grounds. The Deuce also gave up his grandfather's other, more visible means of gaining the "consent" of his workforce, the anti-union thuggery of the 1930s. In 1937 four leaders of the United Auto Workers had been handing out leaflets headed "Unionism not Fordism" when they were brutally beaten outside the River Rouge plant. In 1949, Ford and one of the victims of that attack, Walter Reuther, agreed to terms that became a model of collective bargaining, and a sign that capitalism could serve everyone's interests. In return for the company providing full pension benefits, medical and hospital insurance and wages linked to inflation, the union contracted to provide five years of industrial peace. Soon after, Chrysler and General Motors also gave up their union-busting and put their names to the agreement. It became known as the Treaty of Detroit. *Fortune* wrote that the treaty "made the worker to an amazing degree a middle-class member of a middle-class society."

Impressed by Roosevelt's New Deal in the 1930s, Walter Reuther became an anti-communist social reformer – an American social democrat – and an irresistible (and incorruptible) force in both the union movement and the Democratic Party. In 1948 a shotgun blast through the window of his home put him in hospital for three months. He used the time to work out a better union medical benefits scheme. As Reuther took worker entitlements beyond wages and conditions into pension benefits, health insurance, early retirement and even profit-sharing, he led unions into social reform, civil rights and national politics. He was pushing for the Peace Corps years before Kennedy made it a signature policy. In the early 1960s he urged the big three car companies to join forces and make a smaller, more economical American car. He was close to both Kennedy and Johnson and campaigned for civil rights, both in Detroit and across the country. Brimming with American optimism and bright ideas, Reuther, said one journalist, was the only man he knew who could reminisce about the future. In a parliamentary democracy he might have been elected prime minister.

While busily shaping the American future, Henry Ford indulged a passion for the story of American genius. The Henry Ford Museum of American Innovation is a monument to this appetite. Here are gathered all manner of American inventions and well-earned memorials to the spirit of can-do. It contains, as well, the Lincoln Continental (made in Detroit by Ford) in which JFK was shot, the chair Abe Lincoln was sitting in when John Wilkes Booth crept up behind him with a gun, the bus in which Rosa Parks refused to give up her seat for a white passenger, and a glass jar said to contain Thomas Edison's last breath. Among many other "icons" of American commerce, there is a miniature Ford assembly line, a disassembled Model T, and tours of the Rouge Plant, which these days turns out the country's all-time favourite pick-up truck, the F-150 – a new one off the line every 53 seconds, close to a million sold each year, 136-litre fuel tank, 13 litres per 100 kilometres.

Unsurprisingly, visitors will search the museum in vain for a copy of Henry Ford's book *The International Jew: The world's foremost problem*, any copies of *The Dearborn Independent*, the newspaper he owned and used to spread antisemitic propaganda, or the fraudulent *Protocols of the Elders of Zion* which he published (as did Father Coughlin), or anything commemorating the days when, as well as an arsenal of democracy in Detroit, the company was operating an arsenal of the Third Reich in Cologne.

Jeffrey Eugenides wrote that "most of the major elements in American history are exemplified in Detroit." Race, immigration, the suburban dream, corporate power, class, capital and labour, dream and disillusion, corruption, crime. (The mafia was a persistent presence, but in what big city was it not?) No doubt the same could be said about a few other cities, but for a couple of twentieth-century decades no city came closer to embodying the American ideal. A city of a million and a half people, a mighty manufactory with a spectacular waterfront business district, a powerful and progressive union movement; a young and popular Democratic mayor, Jerome Cavanagh, and a socially progressive Republican governor, George Romney; a city of art and culture from the Institute of Arts' fabulous holdings to Motown, a cultural phenomenon founded by Berry Gordy, who modelled his music business on the Lincoln–Mercury assembly line where he'd worked. Motown was built on the talents of Black songwriters and performers like Smokey Robinson, Diana Ross and the Supremes, Marvin Gaye, Gladys Knight, Stevie Wonder and the Jackson 5. Yet for all their talents, under Gordy's Quality Control, the artists were "a means to an end," the end being the Motown sound. And roughly equivalent to Ford's Sociological Department, Motown hired an "etiquette coach" to make the Black artists more acceptable to white audiences. It worked. Motown moved the world. It also moved Americans, even southern Americans: when Motown artists performed in the South in the early days, the audiences were segregated, but a "common love for the music" changed things when they went back. "People wanted to dance," Mary Wilson of the Supremes recalled. "But when they started dancing, they forgot where they were sitting. And that segregated audience became integrated."

In 1963 the city that gave the world the Ford Mustang and Stevie Wonder united to bid for the Olympic Games. President Kennedy came and enjoyed a tumultuous reception. Half a million, 40 per cent of the population, was Black. Martin Luther King led thousands on a Walk for Freedom down Woodward Avenue, flanked by Reuther, Cavanagh, Rosa Parks, civic leaders, union leaders and church leaders. George Romney would have joined them, but it was a Sunday and he was a devout Mormon. He sent a representative in his place, and a few days later attended a small civil rights march in the exclusively white suburb of Grosse Point. Of course they don't make Republicans like George Romney anymore, and if they did they would be political outcasts like his son Mitt. King's speech turned out to be a rehearsal for the immortal version he gave at the Lincoln Memorial. He called Detroit "a herald of hope."

In the same year, two sociologists at Wayne State University published a seventeen-page study called *The Population Revolution* in Detroit. Hardly anybody noticed, but their research discovered that, on "present trends," the city would lose a quarter of its population over the next decade. Amid all the buoyancy and optimism, Detroit was already on the way down.

*

> *So the real question would be … if people were given the choice between democracy and whiteness, how many would choose whiteness.*
>
> Taylor Branch, quoted in Isabel Wilkerson, *Caste*

Before the Civil War, Detroit was a refuge for runaway slaves. Many were making for Canada across the river. Like Chicago and other cities in the

North, after the Civil War it became a destination for African Americans fleeing the terror and oppression of the Jim Crow South. Not that Detroit was free of racial prejudice. It was one city in what Isabel Wilkerson calls a nationwide caste system, as vicious and thorough in its subjugation of Black Americans as India's is to Dalits and Nazi Germany was to Jews.

In between outbreaks of deadly violence, like Black Americans everywhere else, Black Detroiters were conscientiously excluded from the mainstream as an inferior people. Discrimination in Detroit was structural: it was also, like everywhere else, a daily experience. During the war, Black Detroiters got the worst of rationing, but then they were always the last to be served. When Roosevelt signed an executive order prohibiting racial discrimination in defence industries, and the Packard car company promoted three Black men to work alongside white men on the assembly line, 25,000 white workers walked off the job. It's a moment to go with Wilkerson's argument about caste. Whites and Blacks had worked at the Packard plant for years, but not next to each other. Another day white women came to the assembly line urging white men to walk off the job because Black women were using the white women's bathroom – as if "their fannies are as good as ours."

That was the problem in Detroit. The white folk didn't want to live or work with the Black folk. By 1930, the Black population of Detroit had grown to 120,000. Landlords were already denying them housing in white neighbourhoods. The pattern continued until the vast majority of African Americans were crammed into overcrowded tenements, living in "repulsive conditions" in a few impoverished suburbs. Banks compounded their disadvantage by declaring Black areas "high-risk" and refusing the inhabitants loans. Federal and Michigan state governments completed the process of segregation and discrimination by introducing racial covenants that explicitly excluded Black people from white neighbourhoods: in property deeds, for example, that "said premises shall not, nor shall any part thereof, ever be conveyed, transferred, leased or demised to any person other than of the White or Caucasian race." Prohibited by the Supreme Court in 1948, the method continued to be employed not only in Detroit but across the country, while white suburban associations, in concert with realtors and local government, found other means, including violence and threats, of keeping their communities white. When the federal government made money available for public housing projects, white residents, white real estate agents and white local governments resisted. Seventy per cent of the 45,000 people displaced by highway construction and urban renewal were Black. They were called "freeway orphans."

Escaping death threats in her native Alabama, Rosa Parks moved to Detroit in 1957. Seven years later she said she didn't see "a great deal of difference" between her adopted city and places like Montgomery. For all the efforts of well-intentioned Detroiters, housing segregation was as bad as anywhere in the South. Schools were effectively segregated. In their increasingly ghetto-like suburbs, Black Detroiters endured an intrinsically abrasive 97 per cent white police force, "an occupying army"; discrimination in shops and offices, poor services, daily humiliations. Structural and casual discrimination have a compounding effect. Reducing people to destitution, mendicancy, failure, drugs, homelessness and crime – dehumanising them – makes prejudice into self-evident truth.

"To be a Negro in this country and to be relatively conscious is to be in a rage almost all the time," James Baldwin wrote in 1961. In July 1967 tanks rolled down Woodward Avenue, where just four years earlier King and Parks, with the city's leaders and citizens in tens of thousands, had walked "for freedom." The Detroit riots began with an early-morning police raid on an unlicensed club in the Black suburb of Virginia Park. Five days later forty-three people were dead, thirty-three of them Black; many hundreds had been injured; 1400 buildings were burnt; 17,000 stores were looted; 7000 people were arrested. It had taken hundreds of police and National Guard and nearly 2000 army paratroopers with machine guns to put an end to the violence.

For years a steady stream of white people had been leaving the city for new satellite suburbs linked to downtown by new highways. After the riots the stream became a torrent. Stores closed. White workers, white businesses and white families deserted. They took their dollars with them, leaving the city with a rapidly shrinking tax base. The Black middle class followed. Cars, which had made Detroit a great city, played their part in its fall. Cars being the future, nothing was invested in public transport. Who wanted railways when highways were the thing? Well before the riots, and well before manufacturers began moving their plants to China and Mexico, they had begun to move them to non-union towns. Then Toyota came, with its "lean," "just-in-time" Toyota Production System. Soon the Camry would be the top-selling car in the country, American cars that had epitomised modernity became symbols of decline, and Fordism a relic of an earlier stage of capitalism.

Detroit became heaven for predatory lenders. In 2005, when subprime lending for houses averaged 24 per cent nationally, it was 68 per cent of lending in Detroit – 80 per cent in some suburbs. In 2007 seventy-five per cent of the loans went to Black residents. An avalanche of mortgage foreclosures was the result: 68,000 between 2005 and 2015. The mortgage foreclosures were followed by 100,000 tax foreclosures between 2011 and 2015. Where white people were 17 per cent of borrowers before the 2008 subprime collapse, in 2017 they comprised 58 per cent; though 80 per cent of the population, the Black share declined from 75 to 48 per cent.

Capitalism churned and governance churned with it. Corruption seeped into city hall, the administration and the (rapidly shrinking) unions. Detroit became a shrinking city of the poor, the poorly educated, the unemployed and the unskilled. A city of crime: corrupt in its high places, its streets plagued with violence, theft, arson, prostitution, drug dealing and addiction.

*

Today downtown Detroit belies all the above. The towers positively gleam. The art deco interiors are stunning. The streets are clean, the monuments well maintained. There are cafes and bars. A tram runs down Woodward, making it cheap and easy to get to the Institute of Arts, the Library and

Wayne State. In a city notorious for crime, it feels remarkably … nice, if a bit like a museum. The people are not the unnerving part; it's the absence of them. A bar I found one evening was packed, and it had that feeling of fellowship which all good bars have. It was not a particularly big bar, but it seemed like the entire downtown population was there, and when I walked out onto the empty streets the sense grew stronger. Detroit seemed plain empty, and all the emptier for the acres of carparks where once there must have been buildings. Had all the city workers swept home along the freeways? Or do they work from home anyway? Out the window of the hotel that night the buildings standing in their paddocks of concrete were lit in red, white and blue, but it felt like I was the only person looking at the show.

Drive beyond downtown and the story of Detroit unfolds in images of ruin. Streets lined with long empty, collapsing, weed-infested houses. Places that were once suburban blocks and home to countless families grown over with full-blown woodlands. Ghosts of streets where kids played, and their parents parked their Fords and Chryslers and lived their version of the dream.

Freeways being an American speciality, Detroit's are impressive. They are brutal. Their builders made no compromise with people or with nature and now they evoke the same melancholy as the abandoned factories they barrel past. Some of the old industrial plants are getting a new life as apartments. Artists are moving in. Websites recommend tours of abandoned streets and factories – dress "post-apocalyptic chic." Gentrification is coming to Detroit, but, at first glance at least, it's not convincing.

Of the powerful families of Detroit, two are instructive. Matty Moroun is dead, but the family still owns one of the bridges that link Detroit to Canada. They have done all they can to stop the construction of a new bridge that would compete with theirs. Matty was also, to put it politely, a slum landlord.

Dan Gilbert, a Detroit native and financial genius, is the city's great modern benefactor. He founded the online lender Quicken Loans, which, renamed Rocket Mortgage, became the biggest mortgage lender in the country – "a powerful platform to simplify life's complex moments." He moved the company headquarters and its 1700 employees to downtown Detroit and poured mind-blowing sums of money into revitalising both the business precinct and several suburbs.

A generous giver to good causes, a social visionary and founder and the proprietor of a company consistently ranked in the top thirty "best companies to work for," Gilbert is in the philanthropic tradition of American capitalists that began with the likes of Rockefeller and Carnegie and continued more recently with Bill Gates and Warren Buffett. While the $800-million federal bailout of the car industry helped, and $300 million in federal and private money in 2013, downtown Detroit looks the way it does largely because of Gilbert and the wife of another mogul, Marian Ilitch. With the Democratic mayor, Mike Duggan, they run the city.

"Detroit these days depends on the kindness of strangers," says Steve Babson, a labour historian at Wayne State. He admires Joe Biden for his pro-labour, pro-union commitments, and for the social investment of "Bidenomics." Gretchen Whitmer, the Democratic governor of Michigan and probable presidential aspirant, he thinks "okay," but she is, he says, another corporate liberal, a term he prefers to neoliberal because there is nothing "neo" about the idea of governments doing the bidding of capital. It is not just the prospects for corruption of individuals, parties, cities and democracy itself. Even if the relationships were between parties of impregnable integrity; even if we accept that converting wealth into power is inevitable in a progressive capitalist democracy and needs to be managed rather than discouraged; and even if corporate endowments and investments were sufficient to rebuild cities and communities, how can it be done without replicating the imbalances of wealth, power, education and amenity that destroyed them? By calling his program "Build Back *Better*," Biden at least seems to have grasped the nature of the problem.

For years Steve Babson has campaigned for the rights of tenants under threat of eviction. On average, about 25,000 to 30,000 eviction orders are issued every year. About 30 per cent of those end in evictions. We can assume that the people who avoid these dire consequences nevertheless live troubled lives. Meanwhile, it is hard to see how such people, or the city in general, will be helped by investors buying up suburban properties on a massive scale. Private investors bought one in five of the houses sold in Detroit in 2021. The country's big cities follow the same pattern, if at the slightly less dramatic average rate of seven to one. They "sensed an opportunity," the Ohio senator Sherrod Brown says. Private equity firms and corporate investors "bought up properties, they raised rents, they cut services, they priced out family home buyers, and they forced renters out of their homes." And in doing this they denied poorer Americans, especially poor Black Americans, their one chance to create intergenerational wealth. Private investment has made the already "massive racial homeownership gap" that much wider, and any prospect of something resembling progress towards racial equality even more remote.

Detroit was the definitive American city, the pinnacle of American innovation and industry. For a city like Detroit to fail was more than a disaster, it was a humiliation for the country. American capitalism and American society broke down simultaneously, making the city that symbolised greatness a symbol of failure, an engine of hope, an engine of despair. If you want to know America, know Detroit. If you want to fix America, fix Detroit.

*

There were people in the Institute of Arts, though not what you'd call a crowd. A few years ago, when Detroit declared bankruptcy and a corrupt mayor was on his way to jail, city elders considered selling the institute's fabulous collection to pay off the debt. Two middle-aged women serving in the shop told me they could not bear to think that Donald Trump might get back into the White House. They liked Joe Biden. He was a good man, and they hoped he was not too old to win. What they could not understand was how their fellow Americans could vote for a man like Trump. They thought cell phones and social media might have something to do with it. There is evidence for this: the day after I spoke to them, *The New York Times* reported that regular watchers of the major TV networks were much more likely to vote Democrat. Those who had no interest in the news beyond what is reported in social media were strongly for Trump. These two Democrats felt that the bonds between Americans were breaking. The constant diet of sport and entertainment, the grip of the cell phone, all these screens were dissolving the bonds between people, breaking down communities. In recent months both their churches – one Lutheran, one Protestant – had closed for want of parishioners.

They can't vote for Trump, one of the women said. "Americans are not like that. They're not." You cannot banish hope from the women of the Midwest. Faith and charity – the other two – are also inextinguishable. But what if Americans are "like that"? Enough of them to win. What if they have always been like that?

KALAMAZOO

They did something unusual in Kalamazoo. Back in the 1950s and '60s, when most other towns were emptying their main streets of people and commerce and obliging them to drive miles to newly built shopping malls and strips, in Kalamazoo they made the old main street a mall. As a result, Main Street (Burdick Street) is the main street. There are people and shops and fine old buildings, like the State Theatre, where Homer Stryker, founder of the company that became the Stryker Corporation, once practised medicine, and Buddy Guy and Cat Power are billed to play in June, and the thoroughfare is no echoing museum but more like a community of souls, both past and present.

Kalamazoo (pop. 73,000) is 100 miles west of Detroit. You take the I-94, large sections of which are being vigorously repaired. Apart from the name itself, the town bequeathed to popular culture the Gibson guitar and the Checker Cab; to science and medicine it gave William E. Upjohn's friable pill and Stryker's Cast Cutter, Walking Heel and Circ-O-Lectric Bed. The great paper factories have mostly gone, but Kalamazoo still has healthy industries: plastics, peppermint oil, aerospace, breweries, medical equipment and Pfizer pharmaceuticals (which took over Upjohn). Pfizer's Covid vaccine was made in Kalamazoo.

The little city ranks as one of the best places to live in the United States; top ten in the Midwest for cities with high salaries and low cost of living, top ten in the country for "work-life balance," number three as a city for first home buyers, number two for its job market, three for sustainable development. The Southwest Michigan First economic development agency seems to be one reason the city succeeds. The county is governed by a popularly elected six-member commission, which appoints a manager. A network of neighbourhood associations work with local government to invest federal and state funds in business and community development. They call it "community capitalism."

There is a university, a liberal arts college and a community college: a symphony orchestra, several classical music festivals, an Institute of the Arts and the W.E. Upjohn Institute for Employment Research. There's an international airport, a local newspaper, countless sporting teams and fields, dozens of church congregations and almost as many radio stations. Kalamazoo is one of those towns that seem to live up to America's promise: not all of it, but enough to make any visitor wonder why most towns are not as successful and as amiable as this one. And enough for anyone with a rough knowledge of US history to see in its amenity the long threads of religion, enterprise, education, practical invention and communitarianism – the essentialist philosophy underpinning the old Midwest.

*

Some tornadoes bounce. A Force-2 tornado with 135-mile-per-hour winds bounced along a narrow two-mile path through Portage on the southern fringe of Kalamazoo on 7 May. Among other mischief, it wrecked a FedEx building and obliterated a mobile home. But unlike the Force-3 Kalamazoo tornado of 1980, which killed five people and did $50 million damage, this one left downtown alone and killed no one. Republican headquarters were in no danger. Home for the Kalamazoo branch of the GOP is the basement of an office block in Portage occupied by mental health service organisations. The door, marked KGOP, was locked. No one answered when I knocked.

Kalamazoo is a Democratic stronghold: it voted heavily for Biden in 2020, for Hillary Clinton in 2016 and for Obama both times. A few miles from the vacant Republican office, the Democrats were busy. Though the volunteer women were welcoming, as Democratic volunteer women always are, they had been told to say nothing to reporters, at least not about what they knew or thought about party policy or strategy, or about what they were doing each day. But could they not speak about their own feelings, tell a harmless and sympathetic foreigner something about themselves and what they thought about the state of the nation and Kalamazoo, and how the campaign was going? The oldest of them – she was eighty-six and eloquent – had begun to talk freely to me when a nervous young man appeared from an office to remind her firmly of the vow of silence. Without telling me to leave, he made it clear that it was pointless for me to stay.

Meanwhile, a chap came in with a ladder. Someone had noticed that the flag hanging by the window of the room was back to front: the stars were in the upper-right corner instead of the left. What this might signify no one knew, but in view of the discovery that Supreme Court judge Samuel Alito had hung the flag upside down outside his home to semaphore support for the January 6 insurrection, the Kalamazoo Democrats were in a hurry to get their flag the right way round before a photo turned up on social media and another million people were prompted to believe the Democratic Party was sending secret messages to a shady cabal of idol worshippers and perverts. Next thing you know, Trump would be saying the whole criminal enterprise was "unbelievable."

It was hard to say if the defensiveness – which I'd not encountered at provincial Democratic offices in 2008 or 2016 – was more a symptom of the febrile social media environment or the huge stakes in this election. In any event, it seemed better to admire such far-reaching attention to discipline than be offended by it. Leaving my name and phone number, I departed with a handful of fliers and a list of the Biden administration's "first-term accomplishments" that ran to thirteen pages of dot points.

Burdick Street, Kalamazoo – the mall – is about as accommodating as a street can be. I sat in a café with a bowl of minestrone and read the list of entries. As anyone who ever worked in politics knows, most of the best work goes unacknowledged and mainly unrewarded. The list began: "Addressed maternal health disparities by expanding post-partum APR coverage from 60 days to 12 months in 43 states and Washington D.C. covering 700,000 more women in the year after childbirth." This and a dozen other accomplishments came under the heading "African American issues." Among the others were replacing hundreds of thousands of lead pipes that cause lead poisoning, which "disproportionately affects Black communities"; lowering the cost of insulin to $35, which also disproportionately affects Black communities; likewise, "countering hateful attempts to re-write history," and a string of economic measures to help African American businesses. The Biden administration has cancelled $150 billion in student loan debt for more than 4.3 million people. It has capped the yearly cost of pharmaceuticals for seniors at $2000. It has invested billions of dollars in women's health, and in cancer research.

Then there is the "all-of-government approach to tackle the climate crisis, create good-paying, union jobs, and advance environmental justice." The big tickets are well known: the US has rejoined the Paris Agreement on climate change, and the administration established a National Climate Task Force to cut 2005 greenhouse gas emissions by 50 per cent by 2030 and to reach net zero by 2050. The ingloriously – and puzzlingly – named *Inflation Reduction Act* will contribute 40 per cent of the 2030 target with incentives and investment (upwards of $360 billion) in clean energy. A 2024 environmental version of the Kennedy-era Peace Corps, the American Climate Corps, will put "tens of thousands" of young people to work in well-paid jobs "conserving and restoring our lands and waters, bolstering community resilience, deploying clean energy," etc. The aims, the vision, the sums of money are all heroic. Biden is "on track to conserve more lands and waters than any President in history." He will take care of the Everglades, methane leaks, contaminated mining sites, steelhead salmon in the Columbia River and much more.

If only the environment rated better than a second- or third-order concern in the public mind; if more than 37 per cent of the population believed climate change should be among their government's top priorities; if even half believed that human-induced climate change was a verifiable fact, or that scientists were the disinterested experts they claim to be.

And if only half the population recognised that the US economy is in outstanding shape. It grew 3.4 per cent last year and has continued to grow this year. Fifteen million jobs have been created since 2021, 800,000 in manufacturing, more than in any single year in three decades. 700,000 people joined the workforce in just one month, August, in 2023. Wages are growing faster than inflation. Unemployment is less than 4 per cent. The Dow

Jones has reached historic highs. Why, look at the massive public investment in infrastructure, billions invested in semiconductors, electronics, electric vehicles and much else under the shamelessly protectionist Made in America banner to bring jobs back to the US, guarantee supply and supply chains, and poke China in the eye.

The record *is* impressive. Biden would say that he has led the United States out of the pandemic and into prosperity; that he has led the progressive movement away from the identity politics and "wokeism" that played so well for Trump, and reasserted democratic principle and social fairness. At considerable political cost, he got the country out of Afghanistan, reassured the world's democracies of America's good faith, led the world in support for Ukraine and thwarted Vladimir Putin's ambitions. He might add that he has restored dignity to the presidency. Given that he beat the man who destroyed the respect, the dignity and the trust, and pandered to Putin, Biden has reason to feel that his presidency has been more than a modest success. He might not say it of himself, but he would surely not demur if some worthy or loyal supporter said he has been "transformative," in the way that FDR was and none, including Obama, has been since.

There can be no doubt that from the start he saw a historic opportunity to be such a president – a great one. Four years ago, Biden was the one to hold together a broad coalition – progressives, blue-collar voters, young and old, Blacks, those who subscribe to identity politics and those who do not – to defeat Trump. He had decided to do something no Democratic administration had been brave enough to do since Reagan wiped the floor with Carter and McGovern: to reassert the social democratic spirit of the New Deal: in concrete terms through the Infrastructure Bill, and symbolically by walking a picket line.

He could be his country's salvation, rebuild the country and reset its directions. He could make the United States once again the undisputed leader of the democratic world and immovable bulwark of liberalism. He would remind the Democrats that it is in sweeping social reform that their obligations to minorities and the underprivileged are met. The Black congressman James Clyburn and Black Democratic voters in South Carolina delivered the candidacy to him in 2020 and he repaid them by appointing a Black running mate, a Black head of the DNC, five Black members of his cabinet and more than half of the positions in his sub-cabinet. Half of Biden's cabinet and sub-cabinet are women. His vice president is a Black woman. He is the first president to go beyond the platitudes and set out to prove there is indeed strength in diversity.

Having been made the candidate again, and with overwhelming approval, in May 2024 Joe Biden had reason to think his credentials were singular and beyond dispute, his great mission at least halfway to completion and his place in the sparsely populated halls of great American presidents within sight.

There must have been times in American history when governments did not need to remind the people of their usefulness, but who among the living can remember them? Big business fought Roosevelt's New Deal from the start, and it's still fighting it. Having twice rejected the full-blown New Dealer, Sanders, the Democrats chose Biden to push some New Dealish policies without frightening the corporations or the populace. Yet as president he could have hardly done more to rebuild belief in the power of governments to do things for the general good. He had gone further than most thought he would, and he had managed to drag the party – and major donors – with him, but he had not generated enough enthusiasm and hope to move the polls significantly. In late May 2024 he was, at best, level pegging with Trump, and marginally behind in the battleground states. After three and half years, Trump was a better than even money chance to be president again, the power of the corporations had never been greater, trust in governments never weaker.

Pete Buttigieg, the Transport Secretary (and impressive candidate in 2020 for the Democratic presidential nomination), was once the mayor of South Bend, Indiana, just seventy miles south of Kalamazoo and the old home to Studebaker, maker of stylish cars in the mid twentieth century and electric cars back in 1902. He sees more than an economic benefit in the administration's transport "revolution": the plan has obvious benefits for employment and the environment, but also for the country's housing crisis. Beyond that, he believes that "the future of democratic civilisation will depend partly on ... tangible improvements in very basic experiences," such as efficient transport and the delivery of goods. His plans for a "transport revolution" include a massive nationwide rollout of EV charging stations and a nationwide high-speed rail network on a scale equivalent to the great interstate roads program of the 1950s. When people see things happening, they believe. The January 6 riot, he says, was "fuelled, in part, by a ... belief that our institutions, and the people who lead them, cannot be trusted, because they do not deliver."

Buttigieg might be the ablest spokesman for a transformational core in the Biden administration's philosophy. It may be unfair to Obama and his New Democrat predecessors – it is certainly unfair to Bernie Sanders, who deserves a lot of the credit – but Biden's presidency has been distinguished by renewed belief in the economic and social dimensions of democracy – we might even say, by a *social democratic* bent – and, of course, by Biden's formidable political skills.

Buttigieg is a pragmatic progressive, a believer in "democratic capitalism." He is admirably articulate, as you need to be when navigating from a political position that is at once very sensible and very taxing – and always likely to leave you looking like a mug. For instance, you wish to regulate the corporations so they do not rape society, but since the point is always to encourage their investment and initiative (and seek donations from them), you need regulators whose teeth are not too sharp, nor yet so blunt that the corporations capture them. Your progressive liberal instincts and your popular base tells you the power of money is eroding democracy, the meritocracy is an overrated joke, the environment is too often sacrificed to development, social media is cruelling the minds of the young; and your pragmatic instincts tell you that your party has been up to its neck in all these developments, and that the DNC powers-that-be will never let a Bernie Sanders or an Elizabeth Warren run the show. There are a hundred other pitfalls for "pragmatic progressives" working through the contradictions of capitalist democracies. It would be much easier for people like Buttigieg to go by the name "social democrat," but no Democrat will do that because it sounds anti-business or un-American or foreign, and they figure no one will vote for a person going by that name. But while the term is not precise and describes a variety of political views, Democrat or "liberal" encompass a much wider field without connecting political ideals to social, economic or moral goals.

It is true that the corporate power, feared from the very beginnings of the Union, is unlikely to be banished. But it can be contained for a while. Likewise, social amelioration is possible. Much as they like free enterprise, self-reliance and the American dream, communitarianism comes as naturally to them. Mark Twain, Will Rogers, Helen Keller and Walt Whitman were all American heroes, and all progressive, in some things even radical, in their politics.

Even when he veers from the neoliberal orthodoxy of the past four decades, Buttigieg is careful to press certain familiar buttons: he never fails to praise the innovative genius of the private sector, including its genius in marketing. It is America, after all, and therefore Biden's massive Infrastructure Bill will do its patriotic duty and "help America win the twenty-first century." He strings together new technologies that echo with the old American themes of invention and knowhow – "Tomorrowland – Promise of things to come," as they used to say on *Walt Disney's Disneyland* every week: "self-healing" road tarmacs, asphalt that recycles carbon dioxide, a solar roadway, ultraviolet disinfecting of public buses and trains, suborbital space flight. Buttigieg insists that governments must direct innovation towards socially equitable ends and the public good. In a speech in January 2022, he reminded his audience that while private innovators and marketers invented the world-changing smartphone, the microprocessors, lithium batteries, touchscreens, GPS and the internet on which the phones depend were either invented in the public sector or supported by it; that Google, Apple and Tesla all began with public subsidies and loan guarantees; that the roads, railways and airports, and the regulations necessary for their safe and effective functioning, are down to the public sector.

Biden and Buttigieg *and* further to the left "democratic socialists" such as Sanders, Alexandria Ocasio-Cortez, the Black Marxist academic Adolph Reed and Detroit's Rashida Tlaib might be encouraged by recent polling which showed that, while Americans overwhelmingly believe in private enterprise, just on 50 per cent of people aged eighteen to thirty-four were in favour of socialism – vague as the term is. But a poll in late April 2024 showed that 62 per cent of the same age group were "dissatisfied" or "very dissatisfied" with the choice of candidates, and 68 per cent thought Biden had failed as president.

If only he was not eighty-one and looking increasingly doddery, more and more like a man with degenerative disease, probably some form of Parkinson's. By the end of May, polls showed more than 70 per cent of Americans believed he was too old. In ten days, I had not met anyone "on the street" from the other 30 per cent, not one who thought Biden a good candidate or a better-than-average president. Of course, Trump supporters said he was senile, he and his family were corrupt and the country was going to ruin because of him. But people who disliked Trump also groaned at the mention of Biden's name and reckoned they were both bad candidates. Joe Biden, in other words, was not cutting through.

In the shade of a tree, I was thinking there are surely worse places to live – four-bedroom house on two acres, $500,000; New York an hour and forty minutes, Chicago an hour's drive, London and Paris eight hours; bookshops, library – when the main man from the Democrats phoned. It turned out that the chair of the Kalamazoo County Democratic Party did not share his colleagues' concerns about talking to me. He is thirty-two, Latinx, has a master's degree in public health from Yale and is gracious, open and articulate. Last year he ran for a seat in the Michigan Congress but lost to the incumbent Republican.

He believed the Democrats' social programs will decide the issue in November and doubted the value of celebrity endorsements. He saw Biden trying to reverse the social damage done since Ronald Reagan. The president's age was a problem, but the greater one was a widespread view that the Democrats have been as bad as, if not worse than, the Republicans. Doorknockers encounter people who believe the Democrats at best share responsibility for the country's problems, at worst have betrayed communities by attaching themselves to big money and policies that reflect corporate interests. Campaigners could not tell an unbroken story but must pitch Biden as a man who has set a new course. If Trump wins, he said half-jokingly, Australia should prepare for a torrent of US migrants. The good news for those of us who cling with pride to our traditionally secular ways is that the torrent will not carry many evangelical Christians. The number of Americans professing Christianity has dropped in recent years, although the evangelicals remain a force in rural USA. Campaigners say that while not everyone is of the creed, they all have a cousin or a friend who is.

And if Trump loses? He has not said he will accept the result. He has said there will be a "bloodbath." In Kalamazoo the Democratic chair thought the Proud Boys and their ilk might be more circumspect, and Trump will not want to go to jail for inciting insurrection again. But it worried him that there are heavily armed militias of various sizes in every second or third county across the country.

It's not all like the mall on a sunny day. As it did elsewhere in the US, gun violence in Kalamazoo increased through the Covid-19 pandemic, and almost doubled in 2023, when there were a record twenty-seven murders in the county. (Massive increases in gun *sales* were also recorded across the country during the pandemic.) The Kalamazoo police think the increase is in part a consequence of Covid making it difficult for people to escape family tensions. They also think social media might be inciting acts of revenge. Both interpretations seem at least anthropologically sound, especially when we add to the mix a profusion of deadly weapons and the inability of social welfare bodies to fulfil their usual relieving role during the pandemic.

Vengeance is also on Donald Trump's mind, or so he says.

When the news broke that a jury in Manhattan had found Trump guilty on all thirty-four counts, Solomon saw straight through it, and he reckoned the American people would see through it too. They would see it was "not fair" to go after a candidate like the Democrats had gone after Trump; with a Democrat judge whose daughter was a Democrat fundraiser. And a New York jury. Solomon was from Detroit.

Biden had got away with having classified documents he should not have had, and his son was getting away with all sorts of bad stuff. Trump might drop a little bit in the polls, but when people realised what had happened in that courtroom he would go up – big time. It would be like what happened to Bill Clinton. He went right up when people realised what they were doing to him.

Solomon didn't think Biden would be the candidate. The Democrats had planned it so Trump was convicted. Then they brought on the debates early, so all Biden had to say was – "Look at him! A convicted felon!" The Democrats would watch and if he sounded old and feeble, out he'd go. But they would "shoot him up with whatever they're giving him," and he'd probably seem alright for a couple of hours, then he'd go back to how he really is. In his script Solomon chose plot over character.

The Democrats want Gavin Newsom, he said. Newsom is smart and a fast talker, but people don't want the country to be like California. He asked me what I thought. When I told him where I came from and that I was just watching, he seemed impressed. "Australia! Really! You got Sky News. You're lucky, man. Sky News is what I watch. I don't trust American channels. Sky News gives you both sides."

Whether his outlook was shaped by Fox cum Sky News or by the conditions of his life as a hardworking Black man, by class or race, or a natural sympathy for underdogs, Solomon had the world sorted. In other words, he was near enough to being a typical voter, which means, among other things, that he saw no need to read the policies. And why would he? The media doesn't; or if they do, they don't let it distract them from the relentless evolution of the Story – the Race. That's where the drama is, and the advertising revenue. Citizens don't get policy, and don't expect it. They don't want it. Their minds, quite possibly, are no longer capable of processing it. Trump knows this: he might even know the truth in Umberto Eco's late-twentieth-century prediction that the Good would soon have no connection to Ethics, but rather to the Seen. As the American commentator Mark Danner said, he "commands the true currency of our time: the public gaze." Trump is the human incarnation of the Seen: the internet and the television screen. He is both medium and message.

The Republican Party platform consists of a preamble that inserts "President Trump" firmly in the pantheon of American greatness (defeated the British Empire, "vanquished Nazism and fascism"), twenty promises, several of which sound like they have been clipped from a Trump rally, and ten brief "chapters" under headings in the same vein as the promises. To take a sample:

1. SEAL THE BORDER, AND STOP THE MIGRANT INVASION
2. CARRY OUT THE LARGEST DEPORTATION OPERATION IN AMERICAN HISTORY
3. END INFLATION, AND MAKE AMERICA AFFORDABLE AGAIN
4. MAKE AMERICA THE DOMINANT ENERGY PRODUCER IN THE WORLD, BY FAR!
7. STOP OUTSOURCING, AND TURN THE UNITED STATES INTO A MANUFACTURING SUPERPOWER
8. LARGE TAX CUTS FOR WORKERS, AND NO TAX ON TIPS!
9. DEFEND OUR CONSTITUTION, OUR BILL OF RIGHTS, AND OUR FUNDAMENTAL FREEDOMS, INCLUDING FREEDOM OF SPEECH, FREEDOM OF RELIGION, AND THE RIGHT TO KEEP AND BEAR ARMS
10. PREVENT WORLD WAR THREE, RESTORE PEACE IN EUROPE AND IN THE MIDDLE EAST, AND BUILD A GREAT IRON DOME MISSILE DEFENSE SHIELD OVER OUR ENTIRE COUNTRY – ALL MADE IN AMERICA …

There is another policy document of much greater length and substance which was put together by the Heritage Foundation, a hundred other right-wing organisations and many people who served Trump as president and with whom he has continuing close associations. The president of the Heritage Foundation is Kevin Roberts, an ally of a major Trump donor, Tim Dunn. Dunn has a vision of a MAGA government as the instrument of God's "wrath on evil." Roberts speaks of a new "great awakening" in which the US comes to God, and God's law becomes "a huge influence on the civil laws." When the Supreme Court resolved that President Trump was immune to prosecution in the courts, Roberts declared: "We are in the process of the second American Revolution, which will remain bloodless if the left allows it to be."

Though Trump recently disavowed the document – known as Project 2025 – many of the plans it describes overlap with the Republican Party platform. In 2022 Trump told a Heritage Society dinner that it would "lay the groundwork and detail plans for exactly what our movement will do." The central premise of Project 2025 is a second Trump administration, and the central goal is to grant the office of the president more powers than any peacetime president has had. The document makes clear that Trump is their man; so clear that in his darker moments he might wonder if they don't believe that he is their catspaw.

In fact, the document is there to keep Trump faithful to the hard right, which is no small task in a country as complex and, despite everything to the contrary, as democratic in law and spirit as the United States. It is one thing for Hungary, Italy and Belgium to cross over; for Trump to have taken America to the edge is much more remarkable, though whether it is down to his skills or to the flimsiness of the democracy will be forever open to debate.

Project 2025 decrees that the president will be granted unprecedented powers over the Department of Justice, a standard autocratic procedure which bodes ill for its ability to conduct investigations free of political interference. Schedule F of the document declares a Trump administration will immediately fire thousands of civil servants and replace them with people vetted and approved by Trump's loyalists. In May they had a database of 4000 on the way to 20,000 trusted substitutes. Where Project 2025 does not literally copy the plan used by Viktor Orbán to impose autocracy on Hungary in 2010, it mirrors his example. Trump is an open admirer of Orbán and recently had him as a guest at Mar-a-Lago.

If implemented, even half the plan would create something very like an autocratic US government and, taken with other recent statements, particularly concerning abortion and the Supreme Court's overturning of *Roe v. Wade*, in certain ways a theocratic one. Environmental regulations will be swept away; programs to boost diversity in workplaces will be abolished. Project 2025 can be read as a policy document and a step-by-step blueprint for the first 180 days of a second Trump administration. It can also be read as Donald Trump's instrument of retribution, not forgetting that, in his own words, he *is* the people's retribution.

Retribution on Democrats, on the Republicans who betrayed him, on dud appointments he made, on departments that he believes failed him, on his critics, on the law, on those who "stole" his 2020 election, on unfaithful donors. "Retribution" has gone into his rally language. His audiences roar their approval when they hear the word, just as they do when he talks about vermin. Trump's language might be vague and even incoherent, but like those of every good revolutionary propagandist, his words are never abstract. His killer words are concrete and familiar. He speaks for them, as if by miraculous power he is *in* them. His rallies do have something in common with the revival meetings of the Great Awakenings.

It might be a kind of mimetic desire: what he wants they want; the more brutal his terms, the more frenzied their responses. Or is it that in post-heroic America – the America not of Philip Marlowe or Amelia Earhart or Helen Keller, but of Rabbit Angstrom, car salesman, or Frank Bascombe, real estate agent, or Homer Simpson, halfwit – Trump's pouting plastic face is the only one you can put on the wall of the Men's Shed?

The fact that half the voters in a country that never stops calling itself the world's greatest democracy are cheering on a man with contempt for the law and unashamed autocratic ambitions may be explained by the man's charisma, or by his supporters' derangement. Take your pick. Maybe they all just want to have a good time. To be sure, in 2020 he not only lost the Electoral College vote but also the popular vote by several million. That those millions didn't translate into a more comfortable victory for Biden speaks for flaws in the democracy – specifically the Electoral College and the first-past-the-post, winner-take-all voting arrangements that compound polarisation and the disenchantment on which authoritarians feed. But 74 million Americans did vote for Donald Trump in 2020, and at least as many seem certain to vote for him again this November. They are going to vote for an aspiring autocrat and convicted felon.

At the very least, that suggests half the American population have no respect for their country's laws, and little more for democracy. It was in December 2023 that Trump said he would be a "dictator" on the first day; 2022 when he talked about "termination" of the constitution. The polls recorded no discernible effect. Should anyone be surprised? Old-school Republicans will tell you that before it is anything else the United States is a republic, and the failings in the democracy reflect the effort needed to create and maintain it. It is not a more perfect democracy that they seek, but a "more perfect union." More perfect capitalism, according to one Trump adviser. The United States is also something very like an elective monarchy: the extra clout Project 2025 intends will be heaped on a president who already has more kingly powers than any possessed by a European monarch. American democracy coexisted with slavery for most of its first hundred years, with terror and segregation for the next hundred, and with segregation and discrimination still.

The Republic is an empire whose vast reach is unknown and beyond the influence of most American voters. Expansion was vital to keeping the Republic intact and the idea of America alive. Jefferson and Madison knew this, James Monroe knew it, but those three presidents never imagined the United States maintaining 800 bases in seventy countries, with a military budget that represents 40 per cent of worldwide military spending. The Pentagon operates in a secret and unaccountable realm divorced from the people and their democratic institutions. It has built its unassailable perch on fear and ignorance. Much that happens to American communities, and much in the world that Americans see reported, is a consequence of imperial, not democratic, operations. 9/11, for instance. The exodus from the Middle East. The exodus from Mexico and Central America.

The irony of the Replacement theory is that just as American actions were primarily responsible for precipitating the great wave of refugees reaching Europe, they have much to do with the hordes of desperate people arriving at the border with Mexico. The consequences of US political and military interference aside, climate change, which Trump and his backers do not believe in and will do nothing to mitigate, is credibly held to be making lives unliveable in Central America. Managing an empire not only swallows great sums of money that might otherwise be spent on domestic needs, it also diverts presidents and administrations from their domestic responsibilities. Empires, as Teddy Roosevelt knew, are great for igniting patriotism and national solidarity. As Barack Obama and Hillary Clinton learnt – or should have learnt – they are just as good at compromising democratic values and lighting nativist rebellion.

Alexis de Tocqueville knew something else. He thought the problem might be that democracy promised people more than any society could provide. In granting them the liberty of kings and queens, it seemed to grant a right to have everything that kings and queens had. Democracy can pretend, with words and ritual, that by its release of human creativity it can conjure belief and hope and reverence and deliver on more promises than anything that has gone before it. But it can't deliver to everyone all the time. An election is democracy's effort to outrun the anger and envy arising from its failure to honour the promise of a fair shake for everyone. Trump's magic works because the neoliberal policies of the last forty years are exhausted and disgraced, and the new technology its regime conjured, while making a few mainly unlovely people obscenely rich, does not leave people feeling their lives are easier, richer or safer. The United States sometimes feels like a country, and at other times like 350 million sovereign individuals variously following their dreams or trying to survive. MAGA is 70 million of them handing up their sovereignty to Trump and the movement for the feelings of power that American democracy has denied them. They have been, as it were, dethroned. When Trump abuses and demeans his opponents and all those who are not with the movement, when he dehumanises refugees and immigrants, the MAGA folk feel the power flow through them. Fascism makes the weak feel strong. Those MAGA hats arm them with the power of belonging, grant coherence to their grievances and assert their status as the real Americans. They cry freedom because at last they are safe from it.

Much else in the United States is at odds with democracy. Forty-five to fifty thousand people, including 2000 or more children, are killed with guns every year. Those figures go with the four democratically elected presidents shot dead, several others who survived attempts, and the candidates and civic leaders gunned down. The daily threat of gun violence reaches from the highest office to the streets and schools. The US citizenry is heavily armed with automatic weapons. Whatever the good intentions of the federal government, the states make laws about guns and who can have them.

The states also make laws determining women's reproductive rights, and for political convenience Trump has said he will leave the matter with them. The states find ways to gerrymander electorates and suppress voter registration. States decide matters of education. As the sage Midwesterner Marilynne Robinson reported last year, in Iowa they legislated to protect children in libraries from "woke indoctrination," while also making laws granting the right to carry guns, open or concealed, without a permit. In Iowa, where the minimum hourly wage is $7.30, in the name of "freedom" the Republican government is dismantling labour laws enacted many years ago to abolish child labour. Is Iowa regressing, or just Making America Great Again?

It must be that people living in the world's greatest democracy – or any democracy – have retained, if not an actual affection for the undemocratic, a tolerance of it. We all want to see things getting done, and if they're to our liking or our advantage we don't care if they are done by fiat, corruption or popular vote. No one put it better than Trump did, when speaking of Hungary's "fantastic leader" Viktor Orbán: "He says, 'This is the way it's going to be,' and that's the end of it, right?" Orbán is an autocrat, a kleptocrat and an ally of Putin. No one admires him more than Trump. And Trump shares his admiration for Putin.

You can believe, like 80 per cent of Americans, that democracy's the best system: you can believe it because you were taught it at school, or because you sense the possibilities in it, the restlessness and ambition it contains, but it's that same inherent potential which leaves you open to a leader who bypasses the laws and any other niceties to get things done. This view is as common to Democrats as it is to Republicans.

Republican and Democratic voters express much the same attitude to political violence: when asked, they say they oppose it. But a survey found that 46 per cent of Republicans reckoned the 6 January 2021 violence was an act of patriotism, and 72 per cent disapproved of the House committee that investigated it. This tribal, polarised world seems to be where we are now – and it is very bad for democracy.

The same goes for voting in a presidential election: you might think the guy's no better than a skunk, but you vote for him because he's your guy and not theirs. He's your guy because he'll be better for business, say; and better at dealing with the immigrants; better at keeping gas prices down, telling the Chinese where to stick it and, come to think of it, a dozen other things, some of them not so well defined; like you sense he thinks the way you do, about liberals for sure, but also about, say, preachy women. And Black people.

*

Thirteen per cent of the US population is Black. Thirty-seven per cent of the 1.8 million people in US jails are Black. Forty-eight per cent of people serving life or life without parole are Black. Black people are between two and three times more likely to be arrested by police who are several times more likely to be white.

Twenty per cent of US soldiers are Black: only two of the forty-one most senior military commanders are Black. Two per cent of partners in US law firms, 3 per cent of the Foreign Service, two of the 417 economists at the Federal Reserve are Black. One hundred and eighty-six of 15,000 McDonald's franchisees are Black. One in five people in predominantly Black communities in Los Angeles were infected with Covid; in white Santa Monica the figure was one in twenty-three. Black Americans were almost three times more likely to die from the disease.

Hundreds of such statistics point to the underprivilege of Black Americans. Black (and Hispanic) women are twice as likely to be stuck in low-paying jobs. Murders of Black people are less likely to be resolved. Black people are three times more likely to be shot and killed by police. (More than 5000 people were killed by police between 2015 and 2020.) Black Americans sentenced to death are much more likely to suffer a botched lethal injection. Black people are much more likely to breathe polluted air, drink polluted water or live close to hazardous waste in unshaded streets. Living in substandard neighbourhoods, their children are more likely to attend – or fail to attend – substandard schools.

Race, which is a social construct with no meaning in biology, distorts American society, corrodes the democracy and haunts the American mind like an untreated psychosis. In the society it is expressed in structural segregation, discrimination and persecution. In the democracy it's in the filibuster, state interposition and nullification of federal law, voter suppression – the various means by which the old slave states have kept white supremacy alive – and segregation and policing have maintained it elsewhere. The mind expresses it in all the petty, intimate and destructive ways that Isabel Wilkerson and many others have documented, and in the history that the country cannot live down.

"Freedom" is one of America's essential words. Republicans and Democrats alike stuff it into speeches, paste it on billboards and post it on social media with never a care for its deeply ambivalent meaning. The Heritage Foundation's chief advocate for authoritarian government, Kevin Roberts, calls his *Kevin Roberts Show* "a weekly rallying cry for lovers of freedom everywhere." The Puritans came seeking freedom, and very soon John Williams and Anne Hutchinson were escaping their tyranny. The founding fathers wrote eloquently of freedom even as they asserted their right to own slaves. All through the nineteenth century freedom was inseparable from domination – of African Americans, native Americans, Chinese coolies, southern Europeans, of women. Freedom went with greed and greed with the domination of white men. Therefore, in the vice president, a woman with a Black father and an Indian mother, the country has a potentially transformational figure on the cusp of power.

Like other empires, the United States put down the roots of its empire in the name of every American's right to pursue his interests freely. American imperial adventurers and rapacious companies plundered Central America. Their government seized the Isthmus of Panama, as the New York newspapers said, for sordid mercenary reasons, but also, as the politicians said, to prove the superiority of the "pure white American race" over the "mixed Hispano-Indian race." Teddy Roosevelt said it was necessary for the United States to conquer the Philippines to "secure the greatness of the Nation – the greatness of the race." Mark Twain protested, and millions doubtless thought it was a fair point that he made. But in the end, you had to give it to Teddy, he got things done.

Trump has always been a racist. The justice department sued him for racial discrimination in the 1970s: among the department's grounds, that "the company had required different rental terms and conditions because of race and that it had misrepresented to blacks that apartments were not available."

Telling an audience in Minnesota, a famously "Nordic" state, that they had "good genes" came naturally to a man who has talked about his own "good genes" since the 1980s. In newspaper advertisements in the 1980s he called for the execution of the Central Park Five (Black and Latino men accused of rape) and refused to apologise when they were exonerated, or to accept the DNA evidence that established their innocence. The "Birther" campaign he ran against Barack Obama was based on an obvious falsehood, but proving Obama was born outside the United States was never the point of it. By the time the president produced his birth certificate, Trump had established a fanbase of millions of American voters who were excited by a man so willing to kick the racist can. Aware that white Americans living in areas with increasing ethnic diversity are more likely to be sympathetic to racist dog-whistles and authoritarian solutions, by subtle and not so subtle means he has burnished his credentials ever since.

*

The taxi driver had braces on his teeth. He spoke in a loud, squeaky voice. The car was a hybrid Toyota: the Fords and Chevys are long gone. He was Latino and lived in Queens, close to JFK. Very quiet neighbourhood, he said. He "loved" New York. But the traffic was bad. We had been stationary for ten minutes.

Is the traffic bad in Australia? he asked.

A few streets.

Worse yesterday, he said.

Because of the Trump trial?

Yes, he said.

What did he think of Trump? He liked him.

What they did was disgusting and they'll pay for it. Trump has ideas. He cares for America. You know, migrants live in good hotels in New York – for free! Did you know that? We pay for them. Trump will get them out. Trump will fix. Crime is bad in New York. Trump will fix. He will make America great.

You sound angry, I said.

I am very angry, he said. Americans are very angry.

Near the hotel, we edged past a stationary removal van. One of the two white men loading it walked over, rapped on the driver's window, and shouted, Hey! You be fuckin' careful or I punch your fuckin' face in!*

---

* This next bit didn't happen. Not then, in that street, with me there.

The driver said, You talkin' to me?

As he said it, I saw him reach for something under the car seat, and next thing the window explodes and the removalist is tipping backwards with a stupid grin on his face and a hole an inch wide between his lovely blue eyes.

The driver drove on.

What was eating him? I asked.

Doesn't like his job, I suppose, he said.

Didn't like it, I said.

There was a man in a Trump mask and a Trump suit and a Trump red tie walking up and down among the cars outside Trump Tower, directing traffic with Trump gestures, bumping fists with passing taxi drivers. Most of them seemed pleased to see him, even if it was a fake. A lanky and dishevelled veteran of the January 6 uprising in a MAGA hat was holding forth to anyone who cared to listen. Tourists were filming, of course, and a couple of carloads of cops were watching.

Social media swarmed with threats of violence after the jury found Trump guilty on all thirty-four counts. Trump was a martyr. Biden was a fascist. The Democrats might be tempted to drop their "saving democracy" line, until they can be sure that enough people think it's worth saving. Fox and MSNBC were equally predictable. The Fox people thought most of the convictions would be overturned on appeal, and the judge either would not, or had better not, send him to jail. They contained their glee on MSNBC, but you could see it just the same. Some reckoned the judge would send him to jail. Some that jail would make him a martyr and even more dangerous. Nothing they could say or do on either channel could match the courtroom drama: the psychotic sad sack, Cohen; the temptress and wise broad, Daniels, who started out as a poor girl from a broken home in Baton Rouge and found herself in a Lake Tahoe penthouse with some billionaire in his boxer shorts called Donald Trump.

"When someone hurts you, go after them as viciously and violently as you can," Daniels' lawyer read from the defendant's bestseller, *The Art of the Deal*. The defendant had said all the women on his television show

The Apprentice had flirted with him. He put it down to a "sexual presence" he had. Stormy had a presence of her own. Trump's lawyer accused her of monetising her fame. "Just like Mr Trump," she said. On Truth Social Trump had called her a "human toilet." She tweeted "the best instrument to flush that orange turd down."

The night after the verdict, Trump went to the wrestling; not the old fake stuff, but UFC – Ultimate Fighting Championship. Son Eric and his wife Lara and Trump's valet Walt Nauta were among the party. Walt's up on the same conspiracy charges as his boss over the classified documents found at Mar-a-Lago. As Trump walked in, the packed house chanted, "Fuck Biden!" Then management put on Metallica's "Sad but True":

> Chosen one, I'm the living proof
> With the gift of the gab
> From the city of truth.

The crowd chanted, "We love Trump," as he took his seat. UFC wrestlers fight behind a wire fence. The spectacle could not be less like the old WrestleMania. It is ugly and bloody. In the front row, Trump leaned forward as one man pulled his opponent's arm out of its socket. Later as the dislocator left the ring, Trump pulled him in close for a few words. He stood and pumped his fist, and they shouted – as they do – "USA! USA!" As he left, they played Kid Rock's "American Bad Ass."

I went up the escalator that Trump rode down on 16 June 2015 when he declared he was running for president. Steve Bannon, who became his campaign chair, said the moment reminded him of the opening sequence in Leni Riefenstahl's film *Triumph of the Will*. "That's Hitler!" he thought.

Triumph of the Will begins with a plane – we're to believe the Führer is aboard – descending through the clouds to the towers of Nuremburg, where his followers wait in orderly but tremulous arousal. It's a reasonable presumption that anyone who sees a connection between the film's portrayal of Hitler descending like the saviour from Teutonic heaven and Trump's ride down the escalator is unmoored. But the film's ethereal opening might capture something of the "spiritual" or "religious" sensation Trump rally-goers seem to experience. And it is true that during the 2016 campaign, a suspicion of Riefenstahl – if not of Hitler – surfaced every time the Trump helicopter descended and Trump strode from it to greet his fans.

Early in July, Steve Bannon gave an interview to David Brooks, the *New York Times* columnist who describes himself as a "classical liberal," though he might just as well be called an embarrassed Republican (or anachronism). Bannon is a right-wing revolutionary, who claims to be influenced by an unlikely variety of writers, from Christopher Lasch to Pierre Teilhard de Chardin. When he spoke to Brooks, he was about to begin a four-month jail sentence for not complying with a subpoena from the House Committee investigating January 6 at the Capitol. He was outwardly unconcerned. What sort of revolutionary isn't prepared to go to jail? Even if it's only four months, and the low-security establishment he'll be held in is not exactly Devil's Island.

"The left didn't have what it took because of the cultural issues and the issues of race," Bannon said. "All that madness that they're embedded in. They had to have open borders. They had to have D.E.I. [diversity, equity and inclusion] … They don't understand that the MAGA movement, as it gets momentum and builds, is moving much farther to the right than President Trump. They will look back fondly at Donald Trump. They'll ask: Where's Trump when we need him?"

Bannon reminded Brooks that MAGA had done three things that had never been done before. It removed a sitting House speaker for the first time in history. It removed Mitch McConnell, the "most powerful Republican … in fifty years." Then it removed "the entire RNC." The movement is made of more than supporters; everyone is an activist. They have bored into the heartland through its community institutions. It is not always clear if Hitler or Lenin is Bannon's model, but the ideological difference is immaterial. What matters is the revolutionary instruction: seize the moment when history offers it – or demands it.

If Bernie Sanders has ever grown tired of talking about "millionaires and billionaires" and "our crumbling infrastructure," he hasn't let it show. Why would he? It twice carried him a long way in two Democratic primaries, and earned him a huge following, particularly among young people. The now 86-year-old senator from Vermont became an unlikely regular on television shows that cater mainly to celebrities. He's still turning up on *The Late Show with Stephen Colbert* and *Jimmy Kimmel Live!* to talk about, of all things, income inequality and socialism. His popularity has something to do with his avuncular, unembellished presence, and something to do with the incontestable facts he trots out.

Incomes *are* more unequal than at any time in American history since the Gilded Age. The top 1 per cent *do* earn more than the bottom 90 per cent combined. Sixty per cent of Americans *do* live from paycheck to paycheck. In 1980 the average CEO of a big company earned forty-two times more than the average worker: the average this century is 350 times. The top marginal tax rate in 1979 was 70 per cent: now it is 37 per cent. The richer you are, the more of your income derives from investments, and the more of your income, therefore, is subject to a mere 20 per cent (capital gains) tax. The worker hourly rate, meanwhile, has increased by a mere 17.3 per cent, despite 64 per cent growth in productivity. And the country's infrastructure *has* been crumbling for years.

The more we look at these and scores of other statistics, the more American democracy looks like an empty shell. Call it socialism, social democracy or a new New Deal, the truth that finally dawned in 2020 had been there since 2008, when Obama should have seen it and acted on it but didn't. There would be no Trump had Obama made American workers his resounding cause, and made the bankers at least seem to pay a price for their rapaciousness. Instead, he "muddled through," in the polite words of Joseph Stiglitz, whose imposing anti-neoliberal credentials Obama rejected in favour of people who had been prominent among the unwitting architects of the Great Recession. Eight years later, Hillary Clinton had her chance to say there could be no democracy without economic democracy, or something of that kind. But if she did, it was not so anyone heard.

The essayist and editor Lewis Lapham was surely right to say, "American history is synonymous with the dream of riches." (And, more recently, of celebrity.) We are not to be fooled by the religious element: the Puritans' "New Jerusalem [was] a real estate development in which God and Mammon held equal interest." Yet it is an American curiosity that polls consistently show the people do like the "socialist" cogs that keep American life turning: such socialised medicine as they have in Medicare and Medicaid, public education, social security, regulations which protect their savings, their houses, their environment and their health. Sixty per cent will even agree that corporations and rich individuals should be paying more tax. In 2016, 60 per cent of Democrats said they had a positive view of socialism. In 2021 the figure was 65 per cent.

Yet until Sanders reminded them, and Joe Biden took it up, Democratic lawmakers were still gnawing on the deregulatory free market bone they picked up in 1990s, as if they thought to let go would plunge them into irrelevance. There were two reasons for this: first, they could not resist the elegant self-affirming fashion for supply-side economics; second, Ronald Reagan's diatribe against government did in fact plunge them into irrelevance for a while. Even if, deep in their progressive hearts, they knew that Reaganomics was just another makeover for the country's ancient cult of money, when Bill Clinton made them relevant again, it felt so much better to belong to the cult than to be on the outside whining about the unfairness of it all. In the middle of a tech bubble and ballooning salaries for the meritocratically entitled, at what kind of Democratic dinner party would conversation turn to the Progressive Era, or hoary old levellers like Follette or Jane Addams?

Trump is made of money. He reeks of it. He is its creature. That one so rich and successful should devote himself to the lives of ordinary people invests the man with holiness and grace. Like the hymn: "Amazing grace, how sweet the sound, That saved a wretch like me, I once was lost, But now I'm found. Was blind, but now I see." And so on. Not that it's all one way: they made him president, after all, and no president ever made so much money while in the job. That's because the constitution forbids it – at least for other presidents. It's more than money, of course: his fans feed his insatiable need for attention, his craving for celebrity, but even that, in the end, can't be separated from the money.

Money drives US politics. Big money opposed the New Deal from the day it began, and it still hasn't given up. Big money – mainly the Koch brothers' – was behind the Tea Party and the Tea Party was the raw material for MAGA. Big money became much bigger in 2010, when, in *Citizens United v. the Federal Election Commission*, the Supreme Court voted 5–4 to allow corporations and outside groups to donate unlimited amounts of money to candidates for office. As the judges in the majority explained it, to do otherwise would be a breach of the First Amendment, which guarantees free speech. What it did guarantee was new ways to buy influence.

From the *Citizens United* decision came the super PACs, through which corporations and unidentified donors – so-called dark money – can direct unlimited funds. In the eight years following the decision, super PACs injected $2.9 billion into federal campaigns, most of it from fewer than 100 donors. The *Citizens United* decision made the old link between wealth and power that much stronger. It made good, disinterested policy and open policy debate less likely. It made a somewhat corruptible political system highly corruptible.

Watching the rallies and the advertisements, you would think that the big issues in this election are borders and immigrants, inflation and wokeness – and the character and demeanour of the candidates, of course – and those questions will very likely decide the result. But the crucial issues for the big donors are very different. Mainly they concern how many billions of dollars will stay in their pockets through tax cuts and deregulation, instead of funding government support for middle and working-class Americans. The same consideration explains why billionaires who said after 6 January

2021 that they would never support Trump again have now changed their minds. Call it greed, sound business practice, commonsense accounting or, given Trump's threats of "retribution," fear.

Not every pitch is as blatant as the one Trump made to the chiefs of twenty fossil-fuel companies at Mar-a-Lago in April – for $1 billion to help him get elected he will give them everything they want in the way of tax breaks, they won't have to worry about Biden's environmental regulation anymore, and he'll go on winding up half the country to believe climate change is a hoax and windmills cause cancer. In May he took the same message to oil and gas honchos in Houston, who reportedly ponied up $40 million. At a North Dakota gathering a couple of weeks earlier, by video he told a group of fossil-fuel chiefs that Biden wanted to "abolish your industry and, with it, destroy our economy and send us into a new dark age of blackouts, poverty and de-industrialization."

Meanwhile the big tech companies are swinging his way, not because they need the money but because, dammit, they hold the future of the human race in their hands, and you can't have Luddites and ignoramuses standing in the way of something like that, fussing over AI, trying to deny the right to free speech on X. Of course money comes into it, but the destiny of *Homo sapiens* is the main thing.

*

When Joe Biden walked onto the stage for the first debate, he was behind in the Blue Wall states of Pennsylvania, Wisconsin and Michigan; only a couple of points behind, but behind. Other states thought at least possible wins six months ago – Georgia, Arizona and Nevada – seemed to be lost. He came on like a man looking for his walker. For the next hour he seemed to be looking for his thoughts, and the words to go with them.

I saw Joe Biden live and up close in Ohio on the last day of the 2008 campaign. The smile was something to behold. It came and went and came again like a lighthouse beacon. It lit up the late afternoon in the outdoor auditorium. His stump speech enlivened every soul, and watching him when he moved among the crowd, Black and white, very old and very young – and this was at the very end of the campaign, when he had a right to be at half-pitch – I thought, "Now I have seen a politician."

Biden's smile is still there but the light has gone out of it. It doesn't carry. It doesn't flash. Age is making it rictus. That was not enough to disqualify him, any more than his shuffling feet should have – except it looked like Parkinson's and you wondered if it made sense to elect someone with a degenerative disease, of which one common debilitating symptom is the loss of voice and speech. But that was speculative. In the debate, 30 million people saw concrete and immediate evidence that without an autocue to guide him, the link between his thought and speech was no longer reliable. That he could not be the candidate was clear after half an hour, around the time Trump said he didn't know what the president just said, and he was pretty sure the president didn't either. Trump, of course, lied from beginning to end. Biden was "destroying our country"; he was the worst president in history; and he, Trump, had it all going so beautifully; "we had the best environmental numbers in history," and now look at it. It's tragic. And the illegal migrants, millions of them, it's an invasion, bringing crime, horrible crime, and drugs, killing our people, taking their jobs; and we had the border closed and he opened it, I don't know why. Why would he do that? He's going to lead us into World War III. Trump was a disgrace, but Joe Biden was the story.

The tragedy was that Joe Biden knew he had a good story to tell, but he was not the one to tell it anymore. Just as he couldn't walk forward, he couldn't project his administration forward. He was becalmed like a barque in the doldrums. Here was this gossamered clown threatening to take the United States into a mire, and the old warrior couldn't fire a shot. The defender of American democracy was powerless to defend it.

The unfathomable thing was how the people around Biden had allowed him to walk out in that condition. Was the whole camp in denial, or gripped by timidity or by an excess of love and admiration? Was it a lack of faith in his vice president, Kamala Harris? An acceptance of the general view, for which little evidence was ever given, that she was untalented, unpopular and unelectable? How did they agree to a debate in which the moderators would not correct or question the lies that Trump was sure to tell? And having accepted these rules and followed them in shameless abrogation of the journalist's duty to find the truth, expose its opposite and press for answers to the questions they ask, why did the moderators not take hemlock afterwards?

Biden made a stronger showing at a rally the next day, but in an interview soon after with George Stephanopoulos, the scrambled sentences and painfully long pauses reappeared. His wife and family and closest advisers apparently thought he did just fine. No one else did. But what to do? For three weeks the columnists filed variations on three possibilities for the Democrats: elect a new candidate at an open convention that might invigorate the party – or reduce it to ruins; leave Biden in place, not because he was a strong candidate but because there was no feasible alternative; or make Vice President Harris the candidate, not because she was the right person for the job but because there was … no feasible alternative.

*

A week after the debate, the polls are showing a dip in Biden's support. It is big enough to make Democrats quake, but not big enough to make Biden think he should throw in the towel. The Democrats are facing a convicted felon, a man who encouraged insurrection, seemed comfortable with the idea of lynching his vice president, wondered aloud if ingesting bleach would cure Covid, thinks the F-35 fighter plane is "literally" invisible and that the way to fix hurricanes is to nuke them while they're still over the sea – and they're helpless. They face a credible threat to American democracy and they're trying to work out who their candidate should be and how to make it happen – or not. So long as Joe Biden is at the top of the ticket, they are like Joe Biden: scarcely able to move or articulate.

People wonder how Christians, people who believe in Jesus and God's grace, can believe in a man so deceitful and full of self-love. But who are we to question God's choice of emissary? If it comes to that, seeing him on the rostrum at a rally, Trump does look a bit like someone who has been put together for some dramatic purpose. He does not look entirely in or of this world. Less real than, say, Lady Gaga.

Trump goes to Pennsylvania, to a fairground outside the town of Butler, thirty-five miles north of Pittsburgh. It's a rustbelt town of 13,000, most of them Republicans. Not that long ago Jeeps and Pullman cars were made in Butler. Trump is not there to persuade them to vote for him, but, as one old Butlerite put it, "to soak in the fervor of his base and build momentum towards a third straight Republican Party nomination." These are his people. He is their saviour. The sun is shining and the stands are full of MAGA folk when Trump takes the microphone.

Six and a half minutes into his usual performance, he's talking about the immigrant invasion when he flinches and puts his hand to his right ear. Blood. We hear screams, shots and see people ducking down. Trump ducks under the rostrum and security guards pile on top of him. By now snipers have killed the shooter. The security guards tell Trump it's time to go. He tells them he needs to put his shoes on. When he gets to his feet, he breaks free of the guards for long enough to raise his fist in the air and mouth the word unmistakeably – "Fight!" A photographer gets the shot, with the flag waving behind him.

It happens so quickly you've barely registered the fact of it before you're disbelieving. Can a bullet just graze an ear without shredding it? He's worried about his shoes? Was "shoes" code for hair? "Wait, let me get my shoes" = "Wait, let me get my hair right. Who's got the spray?" Could anyone, even Trump, in those circumstances see a photo opportunity? Where did that flag suddenly appear from – speaking of Leni Riefenstahl! How did security let it happen? The last one *is* a big one. Over the next few weeks – and years – will even half of the population believe the attempt to assassinate Donald Trump was all the work of a twenty-year-old local misfit?

Thanks in large part to the CIA's ceaseless efforts to conduct conspiracies, conspiracy *theories* abound in the United States. After JFK was killed, a half a mile walk in any direction would find a theorist. That was before the internet. Now you need only talk to the person sitting next to you, or the one next to her, or that perfectly ordinary couple strolling by with a pram. Donald Trump was running through some conspiracy theories – the stolen election, the lawsuits being orchestrated by the Democratic Party to bring him down, the climate "hoax," the immigrant invasion that goes with the Replacement (conspiracy) Theory – when he felt for his ear.

But the analysts and theorists will never see the truth of it. They can examine hundreds of phone camera videos, analyse trajectories, scan the shooter's psychological profile, interrogate the Secret Service officers, and they won't see the hand of God. They won't see the moment for what it was. How else could the kid get on the roof with no one seeing? How else could security identify him as a risk and do nothing? What mortal put a tree between the shooter and the snipers? Who made Trump turn his head at the crucial moment? Trump knew the answer: "God alone prevented the unthinkable from happening," he tweeted.

Sadly he didn't prevent it happening in Chicago a week earlier. Of 100 people shot over the 4 July weekend, eighteen died. God's hand didn't intervene, not even to save the children. The gun lobby and the Republican Party are now inseparable, like the Republican Party and the Supreme Court that recently ruled in favour of bump stocks, which convert rifles into machine-guns.

So, Trump goes to the Republican National Convention in Milwaukee blessed. His mission blessed. The Republicans blessed. "He must be the son of God because," as an evangelical Trump supporter told his congregation, "what happened was inexplicable apart from God." "God spared him for the purpose of calling our nation back to its Judeo-Christian foundation." Hence the words of the prophet on that sign beside the highway: "Unto us a son is given and the government shall be upon his shoulders." What more proof do you need?

"We will fear not, but instead remain resilient in our faith and defiant in the face of wickedness," Trump posts. They love it on social media. Folk post pictures of Trump with the hand of Jesus on his shoulder. Republican heavyweights all hold hands and chorus Hallelujah. It was indeed "the hand of God," Governor Abbott of Texas says. Vivek Ramaswamy says, "I personally believe that God intervened today, not just on behalf of President Trump but on behalf of our country." And Tim Scott, the South Carolina Republican senator, sees it as proof that "our God still saves. He still delivers and he still sets free. Because on Saturday, the devil came to Pennsylvania holding a rifle. But an American lion got back up on his feet." It is, as the executive director of the Baptist Joint Committee for Religious Liberty says, "very problematic theology." But irresistible politics.

Sid Blumenthal writes in *The Guardian* that the assassination attempt has put violence back at the centre of the American life. The Republicans rush to blame Biden for it. The shooter was inspired by Biden's talk of Trump being a fascist and a threat to democracy, they say. "Joe Biden sent the orders," Congressman Mike Collins of Georgia writes. Others blame the liberal media as well. Meanwhile, Eric Trump posts the photo of his father with his fist raised and captions it, "This is the fighter America needs." If anyone was thinking about opposing Trump, they won't be thinking it anymore. He is the man of destiny, and all must abase themselves before his majesty. Even Nikki Haley and Ron DeSantis – *especially* those two. And in a box some distance from Trump's sits Rupert Murdoch, the old toad, looking down on all the errant tadpoles he has spawned. You never know how they will grow up, or if every useful idiot can be contained. He backed DeSantis in 2020 – big mistake. He sacked Tucker Carlson. Carlson, he of the cur-like interview with Vladimir Putin, is in Trump's box. He will address the convention. Fox made Trump politically and, years before, Murdoch's *New York Post* helped make him a celebrity. Murdoch didn't want Trump this time, but he's got him, and his presence is unmistakeably a knee-bending gesture.

In Milwaukee, the Republicans unite around their leader in a full-blown cult of personality. But they save some enthusiasm for his new disciple, the man he's made his running mate, J.D. Vance. Vance has distinguished himself immediately with a social media post: "the central premise of the Biden campaign is that Donald Trump is an authoritarian fascist who must be stopped at all costs. That rhetoric led directly to President Trump's attempted assassination."

Back in 2016, when many liberals were struggling to understand what the hell was going on with Trump, Vance wrote this assessment:

> What Trump offers is an easy escape from the pain. To every complex problem, he promises a simple solution. He can bring jobs back simply by punishing offshoring companies into submission. As he told a New Hampshire crowd – folks all too familiar with the opioid scourge – he can cure the addiction epidemic by building a Mexican wall and keeping the cartels out. He will spare the United States from humiliation and military defeat with indiscriminate bombing. It doesn't matter that no credible military leader has endorsed his plan. He never offers details for how these plans will work, because he can't. Trump's promises are the needle in America's collective vein.

Say that to the mob in Milwaukee and you'll be lucky if you get out alive – as lucky as Mike Pence was at the Capitol. But Trump has made Vance his running mate, so they cheer him all the way to the microphone and chant "J.D., J.D.!" long after he takes it, and all the while the phony open-mouthed smile within the fashionable whiskers grows phonier and you think, surely those fabled hard-nosed Midwesterners are wondering about the character of the man Trump has chosen?

No one, Vance tells the crowd, has endured such "lies, abuse and slander" as Donald Trump. But what a man he is. Death had just missed him by a quarter-inch, yet when he stood up, who was he thinking of? Not himself, but the American people. His country. He said fight for your country. Here is a man – "our once and future president" – who had everything anyone could want. Yet he chose to serve us, the people of the United States. Bullshit given this sentimental sheen is unnerving. How are we to react when the untruth is made true in a cult of personality? The transfiguration of a creep.

You feel a flutter of alarm, even before the wild and predictable cheers. Should we be reasoning it back to the causes? This is what globalisation and neoliberalism have done! Or is this investing the requisite inexpressible perfection in a dictator? Do they expect us to take it seriously? Republicans, Vance is saying, are committed to the "open exchange of ideas." And that's how it should be in the USA, he says. We need "a man who is not in the pocket of big business," he says. Are we meant to laugh?

Some of Vance's lines resound, and not only because, unlike Trump, he has a grasp of formal language. He fits his own experience into the Republican narrative. When he was in fourth grade in Middletown, Ohio, he says, Joe Biden supported NAFTA. While he was still at school, Joe Biden supported a "sweetheart deal" with China which cost millions of American jobs and flooded the country with Chinese Fentanyl. While he was in high school, Biden supported the Iraq War. Biden sent American jobs overseas, and American children to war. Trump opposed all those decisions. Biden supported them. J.D., of course, joined up to serve his country.

Sometimes the hoopla makes you wonder if Americans will ever grow up, and if we don't have more in common with the village people of Albania, or Mars. What is it about their longstanding love of marching and mass rallies? Their hand-on-heart, flag-waving patriotism? They are not the only things that you wonder, of course. What is it about executing people that they can't let go? In Oklahoma they have twenty-five queued up. What is it about tyranny that they can't throw off?

Vance is thirty-nine, has precisely 1.5 years' experience in politics – as an Ohio senator – and, if Trump is elected, will be a 78-year-old heartbeat away from the presidency. James Fallows calls him "a dangerous and fraudulent figure" and the "most deeply cynical figure in current public life." The last is quite a claim. Think Mitch McConnell, Lindsay Graham, Tim Scott, Rupert Murdoch, Nikki Haley, the entire Republican caucus.

Still, he's famous. He has an almost too-perfect story, and he's smart and articulate. His wife is Indian: elegant, austere, un-made-up. She looks authentic, and not entirely comfortable sitting next to D.T., who is smiling down on her husband, his apprentice. Vance introduces his mother, about whom he wrote at length in his book. "Ten years clean and sober," he cries, and rather dolefully she stands, and the Republicans applaud. AA without the anonymity.

The grin might not be the only inauthentic thing about J.D. Vance. The hero of the conservative working class who disapproves of corporate donors is a corporate donor's donation to US politics. As much as he comes out of the Ohio backblocks he comes out of Yale and Silicon Valley, and courtesy of the right-wing libertarian billionaire Peter Thiel, co-founder of PayPal, the data-mining firm Palantir Technologies and many other companies named after the creations of J.R.R. Tolkien. Palantir's $20-billion business is substantially built on contracts with American intelligence agencies, which seems odd for a libertarian. Thiel spent $15 million getting Vance into the Senate and did more than anyone else to persuade Trump to make him his running mate. "I no longer believe that freedom and democracy are compatible," he said recently. "Since 1920, the vast increase in welfare beneficiaries and the extension of the franchise to women – two constituencies that are notoriously tough for libertarians – have rendered the notion of 'capitalist democracy' into an oxymoron."

On the last night, Trump is introduced – as one would expect – by the CEO of the Ultimate Fighting Championship. His wounded right ear is covered by a white rectangular dressing. He shares the stage with the firefighting jacket and helmet of the volunteer firefighter who died shielding his family in the shooting at Butler, Pennsylvania. As he approaches the microphone, a massive slide of the White House descends behind him.

He begins on script, reading the words from the teleprompter "in saintly measure," to borrow Armando Iannucci's phrase. They would have a great victory in November, and the US will then enjoy the greatest years in all its history. To do this we must end this divisiveness. All Americans must come together as one people – and here he sounded like some kind of liberal multiculturalist, but you could see he was reading it, so everyone knew they could relax. Then he's recounting step by step the ordeal in Pennsylvania:

how he turned his head, heard a whizzing noise, felt for his ear, blood, so much blood, ducked down behind the rostrum. Bullets were flying yet he felt "serene" – such a regal word, "serene." "I stand before you in this arena only by the grace of almighty God."

Many in the room are moved to tears, and the others maintain a solemn silence. The media, and by no means all pro-Trump media, describe it as moving. Some among them, even some Republicans, surely, find it merely Trumpian: solipsistic, manipulative and, when he walks across the stage and caresses the jacket and kisses the helmet of the dead volunteer, nauseating and macabre. It's a matter of taste, of course.

It is customary for people saved by God's grace to speak humbly and gratefully – "how sweet the sound to save a wretch like me." But democracy is a restless system. It works through unrest. Trump senses this. He might have been saved but he's not going to act the wretch. After twenty minutes of sounding like a liberal wuss, he throws the switch to American badass, or vaudeville, as Paul Keating used to say.

For the next seventy-five minutes he gives his audience what they are used to: a rambling collection of lies, boasts, exaggerations and childish drivel. Here in the land that gave us Gettysburg the two great parties are led by a man who cannot find the words to match his thoughts, or, if he can, cannot utter them; and a man for whom language is a kind of tip truck with messages, both familiar and coded, saccharine and malevolent, strewn among the garbage. "Let language be the divining rod that finds the sources of thought," Karl Kraus said. You can see that happening in the address inscribed on the wall of the Lincoln Memorial. You won't see it happening with Donald Trump. To be fair, few if any modern politicians treat language as the divining rod of thought – or the mother or midwife, as Kraus called it elsewhere. The game's too fast. It can't be stopped while our leaders go looking for thoughts.

Inevitably Trump riffs on the theme of illegal immigrants. The border is a problem, no question, and the people are right to be concerned. But are the immigrants "destroying" the country? Is it the "greatest invasion in the history of the world?" They're coming from prisons, he says; they're coming from insane asylums. It's a scene from a horror film: rapists, murderers, mad people. A horde of criminals spreading out across the country. "Has anyone seen *The Silence of the Lambs?*" he says. He's dropped this line into many speeches and is beginning to wonder if anyone remembers a film from the early 1990s. "The late, great Hannibal Lecter. He'd love to have you for dinner. That's insane asylums. They're emptying out their insane asylums." In Caracas crime is down by 70 per cent, he tells them. Why? Because they're sending their criminals here. Same with El Salvador. He goes through a list of crimes committed by illegal aliens. Naming their victims and the survivors. I will not let them in the way "this horrible administration" has let them in.

He goes beyond traducing Biden and simply makes things up. He gets the crowd – a Disneyland of bottle blondes and corpulent men in funny hats, those from Wisconsin wearing what look like polystyrene Swiss cheeses on their heads – chanting, "Drill, baby, drill!"

By letting the immigrants in, the Democrats will destroy social security and Medicare. They will take jobs, especially Black and Latino jobs.

He, Trump, created world peace. Joe Biden created war. Russia was afraid of Trump – Orbán said so. Russia took nothing when he was president. Now look. He stopped Putin, and Kim Jong-un: they're frightened of him. He could stop wars with a telephone call. He had no wars, except ISIS and "I defeated ISIS."

He will build an iron dome over our country.

He will find a cure for cancer and Alzheimer's.

He will not let men play in women's sports.

And you're going to be able to drive gasoline-powered cars (*much cheering, whistling and foot-stamping*).

The convention had wrapped him in the garb of a caring father and grandfather, a family man. When the extended family went up on the stage at the end, there was no mistaking it: this was a *royal* family. It was Trump Inc. laundered. Twice impeached by Congress; found liable for sexual abuse and for defamation and for fraud; convicted on thirty-four counts relating to falsifying business records to hide hush-money payments to a porn star; facing numerous federal charges relating to the 2020 election and classified documents found at Mar-a-Lago, many of which (if he is not elected president) carry prison sentences; "a prolific and sophisticated litigant who is repeatedly using the courts to seek revenge on political adversaries … [and] … the mastermind of strategic abuse of the judicial process," in the words of a federal judge; a man who lied more than 30,000 times in his four years as president, Donald Trump was a step away from pulling off an unbelievable heist. Another one. But, to borrow a favourite Trumpian refrain, "a lot of people don't know this." A lot of people are going apeshit with love and exaltation.

For Democrats, Trump's performance sharpens the pain. Not because his performance is convincing, but because it's so relentlessly vacuous and stale. He looks so beatable. In the weeks since the disastrous debate, the polls have moved to Trump by a single point at most. The small percentage of voters who will decide the election have no love for him. If only the Democrats had a candidate who could reliably make the case.

He's been a good president. On Stephen Colbert's show after the RNC, Bernie Sanders says Joe Biden is the best president in his lifetime – and he plans to do much more. It's not because he's incapable of governing, at least for now. But he can't campaign effectively. The interviews following the debate were unconvincing. He lost his way, mixed up names, looked blank at times. It was as if inside his head he knew what was what and who was who: it was all there, but he couldn't say it. With the focus on Biden's infirmities, Trump's blundering goes unnoticed.

A steady trickle of donors, former senior officials and sympathetic journalists and thirty-six Democratic congressmen and women are urging him to step aside. It seems likely that Obama is pushing gently. But Biden says he's going nowhere. His wife, Jill, his family and his close advisers back him. His vice president resolutely backs him.

Nancy Pelosi, she of the "iron fist in the Gucci glove," also backs him, but in private she is telling him he has no path to winning in November. Biden puts out a letter saying there is no decision to be made, the party voted for him to be the candidate overwhelmingly, and he is running. Two days later Pelosi tells MSNBC's *Morning Joe*, "It's up to the president to decide if he's going to run. We're all encouraging him to make that decision because time is running short." She says later her purpose was twofold. She wanted people to back off while Biden was chairing a NATO meeting. And she wanted to defeat Trump. Because it's not like defeating Bob Dole or George Bush, she told Ezra Klein – it's autocracy or democracy. She was telling Biden he could make the decision himself, or have it made for him. She had given him the chance to go with dignity, with his presidential record unfinished but intact, and with every assurance that history will regard him as a great servant of the country, a good president and a decent man. With his legacy burnished or spoiled.

Pelosi has performed a miracle of personal and political adroitness. If anyone is Philip Marlowe in this show, it is Pelosi. But who believes the Democrats can match it? "I don't belong to any organised political party. I am a Democrat," as Will Rogers said. A hundred years later, what are the disorganised to do? There are half a dozen talented governors and as many senators to choose from. That's the good news. It's also a lot of ambition to contain. How, within a fortnight, can they find not only the most capable candidate but the one most suited to the unique demands of a fight with Trump? Who might persuade undecided voters, while not offending the sensitivities of certain Democratic blocs?

Biden makes it easier for them by immediately endorsing his vice-president, Kamala Harris. And somehow, barely an audible whisper of discontent is heard as the Democrats fall in behind her.

She could not have played it better. No one could accuse her of disloyalty – though Trump might – yet she lands at the head of the campaign as if she's always been there. For three years it has been a given of politics, Democratic and Republican, that she was an ordinary vice president at best and could never be the candidate. Trump sporadically swiped at her, blamed her for the immigrant "invasion," yet put little time into her. Even after the debate debacle, he seemed only to briefly muse on the possibility that Harris would be his opponent. Three weeks before Biden resigned, he was filmed, slumped in his golf cart with son Barron next to him, telling a couple of off-camera bystanders that he had "kicked that old broken-down pile of crap" Biden, and he'd pull out and leave him facing Kamala, who was "bad" and "pathetic."

If she had said precisely nothing in the first fortnight, Harris might still have turned the polls around. The smile that used to do it for Joe does it for Kamala in spades. She talked about "joy," and joy does seem to be the dominant emotion at her rallies. The media never registered the darkness that hangs over Trump's rallies, or the gloom generated by a contest between two old men.

It won't help that she's from San Francisco, though Reagan, who remains a revered figure for reasons not everyone can understand, hailed from California too. She was San Francisco's district attorney from 2004 to 2011, state attorney general after that. She won the ballot for attorney general by 0.85 per cent after three weeks of counting, and it's generally believed only because her popular opponent gave one honest but impolitic answer during a debate. Had she lost that election, it's unlikely that she would be running for president now. Most successful politicians have one great stroke of luck in their career. Some have more than one, and Trump might prove to be Harris's second. In her first speech as the candidate, she delivers a defining zinger: she says that as a prosecutor she dealt with a lot of fraudsters, and she therefore knows Trump's type. The part of the electorate that knows her at all recalls her steely interrogations of the Trump-appointed federal attorney general Bill Barr, among others. Interrogating reveals the adamant flipside to her frothy ebullience. She has a sense of humour, which can make life difficult for a man who lacks one. That she's a woman makes it worse for him. The bullying, stalking routine he used in the debates with Hillary Clinton seems less likely to win hearts this time – if, indeed, it won any then. He began saying Kamala is "beautiful," then turning it into culture-war material: you're not allowed to say a woman is beautiful anymore, he tells the crowd – and of course his other audience, social media's infinite realms of the anti-woke. But Harris on a *Time* magazine cover which makes her look beautiful, and Peggy Noonan saying she *is* beautiful (and warm and radiant), sets him off: "She said Kamala has one big advantage, she's a very beautiful woman. She's a beautiful woman." The crowd boos on cue. It's Taylor Swift all over again. How to deal with rejection? Or does he know that he's not the only one to feel it? Is he shooting darts into the jealousy that lurks in the human heart? Then he says: "But I say that I'm much better-looking than her. Much better … I'm a better-looking person than Kamala." And the crowd cheers. In the same speech he will tell them he is smarter, too. He's "really smart." She has a low IQ, he says – repeatedly.

But his first move strikes at her colour. Is she Indian or was she Black? She used to be Indian but now she's Black – meaning she's changed her identity to pick up Black votes. In fact, her mother, who raised her, is Indian. Her father is Jamaican. She has always identified as Black and went to Howard, a Black university. It's of no account to Trump that on the mainstream news he looks like a racist: what matters is that he looks like one when his bait lands on the internet. Then it's the way she laughs: "Have you seen her laugh? … That is the laugh of a lunatic!" At the same rally, where his speech lasted 105 minutes, he says she is a "communist, a Marxist and a fascist." At his press conference on 10 August, an NPR journalist counts 162 lies and distortions and publishes them.

When she ran in the 2019 presidential primaries, Harris's record as a prosecutor was used against her by progressives. She had championed laws to prosecute the parents of "habitually truant" children. While claiming to oppose the death penalty she appealed the ruling of a federal judge that capital punishment was unconstitutional. (At the time 740 people were waiting on California's death row.) She opposed a bill requiring the attorney general's office to investigate police shootings, and another requiring officers to wear body cameras. On more than one occasion she refused to dismiss a case where wrongful conviction had been demonstrated. The lawyer and "zealous advocate" who in 2019 wrote a *New York Times* op-ed outlining these decisions says since Harris became the candidate she has been approached by "every media outlet you can think of" asking her to "comment." On X she "comments" that 2019 is "a lifetime ago," when she was writing into a crowded primary field, and now "all of us need to make sure she wins the Presidency."

Harris's moves so far seem to be subtle and well-judged. She talks about Trump threatening freedom. That word. Democrats and Republicans can now stand on opposite sides of the road and shout "Freedom!" at each other. For Democrats, it means breaking even on the country's favourite word – or delusion, take your pick. But the word has at least one concrete meaning: the freedom of women to control their own bodies.

For a fortnight we waited to see who she would choose to be her running mate. Wise heads said running mates never made a difference, but that didn't stop them wondering. It came down to three men: Governor Josh Shapiro of Pennsylvania, Senator Mark Kelly of Arizona and Governor Tim Walz of Minnesota. Shapiro's claim rested on his popularity in the most crucial of all the crucial states; Kelly's on such impeccable credentials as long service as a Navy fighter pilot and an astronaut, along with his proximity to the border and the beckoning prospect of dragging Arizona back into play for Democrats.

She chose the avuncular, jolly, courtly but surprisingly forceful Walz – a schoolteacher and football coach, a one-time senator, an old-school Midwest progressive who in old people might conjure memories of W.C. Fields. So far, the choice seems inspired. They seem to enjoy each other's company and take pleasure in their shared beliefs and the fight they have joined. There is more to this than soppy liberal boilerplate. The uncanny ease with which first Harris then Walz dropped into the campaign, and the excitement they brought with them has given the Democrats the glow they needed. The tone has changed. Instead of waging war with Trump, for the moment they are transcending him. Transcending Joe Biden's angst as well, it seems – he joins Kamala at a rally, where she pays unrestrained homage, and he gives her his chivalrous blessing. She leaves no doubt that while she may change emphases, the direction will not: a Harris presidency will be a continuation of Biden's.

As the Democratic Convention begins, Harris–Walz have hit the front in the polls, not by enough to entitle any sensible person to feel confident they will win, but they have an even-money chance. Not only has Harris edged in front of Trump in the polls, the Democrats are marginally ahead in two of the three Blue Wall states, and North Carolina, Georgia, Arizona and Nevada are back within reach. "Marginal" is the operative word: they are all within the pollsters' margin of error, but a good convention might push them beyond that. Even in Florida, where Trump loyalists recently staged a rally in their golf carts, the Democrats have climbed back to a competitive level.

But the real tests are yet to come. While the election can be fairly described as a contest between democracy and something more like an autocracy, it is likely to be decided by personalities and the price of gas, and the media will continue to treat it as a glorified horse race. We will best know the decisive issues by referring to Trump's speeches. Nikki Haley and Lindsay Graham, among others, are urging him to stop the personal attacks and sell policies. But policies lead back to Project 2025, which Trump thinks he must disown. In the further reaches, the white supremacist internet "influencers," some of whom Trump has had to dinner at Mar-a-Lago, are dismayed by his unwillingness to go harder on both policy and personality. These people have some clout. But loopy as the man often seems, and allowing for some doubt hovering around the ambitious J.D. Vance, it would be unwise to think he doesn't know what he's doing.

It's like binge-watching a TV series. I've been back in Australia for six weeks, and people seem more interested in the US than anything happening here. Peter Dutton seems to be going well. I find myself wondering if, driving the roads of Detroit and Ann Arbor, Harvinder has changed his mind about Donald Trump. Could the Harris smile or Walz's energy do for him what Trump's daily hand grenades were doing two months ago? Or if a new-made citizen of Indian origin shares with a majority of American "legacy" voters, and virtually all Republicans, the view that Trump – fool, crook or fascist – offers the best hope for their personal prosperity?

The Democratic convention is a frenzied, joyous affair. Biden enjoys a five-minute standing ovation. The lovable Walz, offering an alternative to Proud Boy masculinity, does his football coach routine. Oprah makes a surprise appearance. The Clintons speak: Hillary is cheered, Bill less so, though one observer says he still has the art of "putting the hay down where the goats can get it." It is hard to resist the excitement in the room, but then the Obamas raise the bar a few more notches – and you wonder if American rhetoric has evolved to this level to cover the permanent cracks in the Union and the impossible ambition. "There are no red states or blue states, only the United States of America." Who's he kidding? "When they go low, we go high." Lovely. But remember Sarah Palin? Within six months of Obama winning in 2008, she was inspiring the white working class with "How's that hopey, changey thing working for you?" and with this seemingly pathetic line she got the Tea Party going.

Were there any among the exultant crowd longing to hear Obama or Clinton say they had got a few things wrong? That the New Democrats were no more. That instead of deregulating banks, bailing out bankers and giving the perpetrators jobs in their administration, they might have been contesting the low-income territory that Trump would make his own.

The convention is an orgy of rhetoric, and you're soon left wondering when the crowd will tire of it and demand their leaders say what they plan to do and give the country reasons to believe that they are honest brokers. As usual, the best lines were saved for Donald Trump, which pleased the audience and Trump, no doubt, in equal measure. Nowhere was it reported that the Democrats knew how to fix Detroit, or any other city like it. Shawn Fain, the United Auto Workers boss, put the case for the working class, praised Biden, endorsed Harris and reminded viewers that unions still exist. His red "Trump is a Scab" t-shirt might have been a sane rejoinder to Hulk Hogan's performance at the Republican convention.

Essentially, the convention promised to follow Biden's path. The difference was the candidate. This *is* the miracle of American democracy: out of the chaos and loathing and the seeming impossibility of unity and progress emerges a Black woman radiating joy who just now has a fair chance of becoming president.

There's no denying Harris's appeal. For now, she is defying the poisonous commingling of politics, entertainment and social media, "where the choreographed image or manufactured narrative becomes the only reality we have left," as Armando Iannucci wrote after the Veep became the Candidate. Her case must also survive the debilitating habits of American speechmaking that undermine authenticity by seeking it in tattered cliches of the "only in America could someone like me be president" kind, and the mandatory panegyrics to a wise ma or pa. Yet, allowing for these rhetorical obligations, the excesses of patriotism, and the exceptionalist rants which leave folk in less exceptional places wondering if Americans are not the most provincial people on earth, she gave a terrific speech at the DNC.

It wasn't pretty. It didn't soar. In the end it didn't even say much. Her personal story was not as powerful or affecting as Pete Buttigieg's understated gem. Michelle Obama and Gretchen Whitmer were wittier, A.O.C. more beguiling; the long line of women, including Hillary Clinton at her best and Oprah Winfrey, made Harris's arrival a matter of historical necessity – this time it had to be a woman. Harris has presence, and when she puts aside adornment and slows the flow of words, she is compelling. Even in icy prosecutorial mode, she retains enough passionate conviction to make her threatening. It might be this that seems to have frightened Trump: he thinks she'll eat him.

Just now it seems faintly possible that Trump will melt down completely and the Republicans will have to rush in a replacement. Much more likely, the contest will stay close to the end. The American electorate defies much ordinary understanding, but some might respond if Harris were to say at the beginning of the debate and serially afterwards, that democracy can only function on a firm basis of truth, and Trump's lying is better suited to the

Russia of his friend Putin. Thereafter, keep the love but temper the joy. The people whose votes they need see nothing to be joyful about. Stop talking about the middle class, as if working people have only themselves to blame for low wages, and rents and mortgages they can't afford. If you must believe in the meritocracy, keep it under your hat. In Kalamazoo they want more houses. Same in Detroit. The Democrats have had a miraculous six weeks. Can they now make a concrete case? Make it all about what they will do.

Whatever happens in November, it won't be the end of the story, just the first series. If Trump wins, how far towards Project 2025's objectives will he go? He won't have to go far to trigger protests. He has always said he wouldn't hesitate to call up the military. Would the military obey him? If Harris wins, will Trump accept the result? What happens then? He says a bloodbath. Either result will make for a riveting second series. We should hope that the recent film *Civil War* does not make a third.

But in the end, you find yourself asking why you're watching. You have your own life to lead. Why let yourself be lured into theirs? They're writing the script, and they'll decide the ending. We don't have to watch. There's always the off button on the remote. But what if the ending's like *Little Caesar*'s, with the gangster on top of his tower moaning, "Mother of mercy, is this the end of Rico?"

23 *August* 2024

SOURCES AND ACKNOWLEDGEMENTS

Thanks to Derek Shearer, Sue Toigo, Steve Babson, Judith Thurman, Chloe Hooper and Chris Feik.

3 "legacy in Atlantic City": Will Yakowitz, "Good riddance …", *Forbes*, 5 May 2022.

3 Too bad if a mobster: "Film taken in 1988 shows LiButti ringside as Trump's guest, the mobster's daughter says", *The Huffington Post*, 2 November 2016.

3 "when I get Andre the Giant": Hulk Hogan, WrestleMania IV, March 1988.

8 "broken communities," etc.: J.D. Vance, "Opioid of the masses", *The Atlantic*, 4 July 2016.

9 Two-thirds of Americans: *The Economist*, 22 July 2024.

10 as if still attached to the seventeenth century: Sam Kestenbaum, "The demon slayers: The new age of American exorcisms", *Harpers*, August, 2024.

10 "prepared men": Robert Putnam, *Bowling Alone*, Simon & Schuster, New York, 2000.

10 a symptom, a cause and a solution: Michael Toscano, "Scrolling alone: Smartphones and social atomization", a review of Jonathan Haidt, *Anxious Generation: How the great rewiring of childhood is causing an epidemic of mental illness*, Penguin, 2024, *American Affairs*, vol. 8. No. 3, Summer 2024.

10 millions of Americans retain the faith: Molly Olmstead, "QAnon's victims", *Slate*, 29 July 2024.

11 "legacy Americans": Tucker Carlson, *Fox News*, 22 September 2021.

11 University of Massachusetts Amherst poll: Tim Dickinson, "Poll: Trump and the GOP's fascist rhetoric has broad appeal", *Rolling Stone*, 13 February 2024.

11 "significant market" etc.: Dickinson, "Poll".

12 "Purify society": Henry Adams, *Democracy: An American novel*, The Modern Library, New York, (1880) 2003, p. 42.

15 More than half: Notre Dame News, "On the brink of a new civil war", 3 November 2022, https://news.nd.edu/news/on-the-brink-of-a-new-civil-war-new-national-survey-highlights-fragility-of-american-democracy-stark-partisan-divides/, accessed 23 August 2023.

19 "superb": James M. Cain, "Paradise", *American Mercury*, March 1933, republished, *Los Angeles Times*, 1 January 2012.

21 about 6000 volunteers: Los Angeles Homeless Services Authority, Press release, 29 June 2023. Results of 2024's count have not yet been released.

21 worst state for homelessness: With 122,000 homeless people Australia's rate per capita is a fraction higher than California's, and between two and three times that of the United States.

29 America the eternally hopeful: See, for example, Michael Matthews, *American Ruin: Life and death on the streets of Detroit – America's deadliest city*, Silvertail Books, London, 2019.

31 "Father Coughlin": See David Maraniss, *Once in a Great City*, Simon & Schuster, New York, 2015, pp. 209–11.

34 a shotgun blast: His brother, another union leader, was shot and seriously wounded the following year.

34 the only man: Damon Stetson, "Walter Reuther, Union pioneer with broad influence far beyond the field of labor", *The New York Times*, 11 May 1970.

35 operating an arsenal of the Third Reich in Cologne: Ken Silverstein, "Ford and the Fuhrer", *The Nation*, 24 January 2020.

35 "etiquette coach": Chris Perkins, "How Detroit assembly lines changed music forever", *Roadtrack*, 29 October 2020.

36 "common love for the music", etc.: Mary Wilson, quoted in "Higher ground", *Wax Poetics*, 9 December 2020.

36 "a herald of hope": Romney, a genuine self-made man, presided over the American Motor Corporation, which made the Nash Rambler, the "compact" alternative to cars he called "gas-guzzling dinosaurs" made by the big three Detroit companies. He knew King and was a keen supporter of civil rights.

36 two sociologists: Thomas Ford Hoult and Albert J. Mayer, *The Population Revolution in Detroit*, Institute of Regional and Urban Studies, Wayne State University, 1963.

37 nationwide caste system: Isabel Wilkerson, *Caste: The origin of our discontents*, Random House, New York, 2023.

37 "said premises": Derek Shearer, "Growing up white", *Inroads*, Issue 48, 2021.

39 Where white people were 17 per cent: Jeffrey Wilson and Bambi Kramer, *We Live Here: Detroit eviction defense and the battle for housing justice*, Seven Stories Press, New York, 2024, pp. 5–7.

42 "sensed an opportunity": *The Washington Post*, 16 February 2022. Brown, a Democrat, is chair of the Senate Committee on Banking, Housing and Urban Affairs.

46 prompted to believe: Lest the public think a judge of the Supreme Court – and one sitting on a case concerning Donald Trump's involvement in the January 6 invasion of the Capitol – might be an insurrectionist, Alito told the media his wife had done it. She hoisted the flag in the offending position, he said, after an altercation with the neighbours. But the neighbours said the flag was flying upside down on 17 January, just eleven days after the Capitol rioters sent the same signal with their flags, and the altercation occurred a month after that. Judge Alito said he would not recuse himself from the case. *PBS Newshour*, 7 June 2024.

47 37 per cent of the population: Pew Research Center, 9 August 2023.

49 strength in diversity: See Derek Shearer, "Race and politics in a diverse nation",

Inroads: The Canadian Journal of Opinion, Issue 49, 2021.

52 poll in late April 2024: CNN poll, reported 29 April 2024.

55 "commands the true currency": Mark Danner, "The grievance artist", *The New York Review of Books*, 22 November 2023.

55 both medium and message: Bannon told David Brooks, "I call Trump a Marshall McLuhanesque figure. McLuhan called it, right? He says this mass thing called media, or what Pierre Teilhard de Chardin said of the noosphere, is going to so overwhelm evolutionary biology that it will be everything. And Trump understands that. That's why he watches TV."

56 "We are in the process": Associated Press, "Leader of the pro-Trump Project 2025 suggests there will be a new American Revolution", *Politico*, 7 April 2024.

57 database of 4000: Mark Lilla, "The tower and the sewer", *The New York Review of Books*, 20 June 2024.

57 in certain ways a theocratic one: See, for example, Robert Reich, "The Republican Party wants to turn America into a theocracy", *The Guardian*, 24 February 2024.

57 post-heroic America: See Barbara Ehrenreich's review of Richard Ford's *Independence Day*, *New Republic*, 19 September 1995.

58 More perfect capitalism: Thom Hartmann, "Are our oligarchs going to drag us into civil war?" *New Republic*, 20 May 2024.

59 climate change: Alfred W. McCoy, *To Govern the Globe: World orders and catastrophic change*, Haymarket Books, New York, 2021, p. 290.

59 Barack Obama and Hillary Clinton: McCoy, *To Govern the Globe*, pp. 246–49.

60 Fascism makes the weak feel strong: Eric Fromm drew a link between fascism and Calvinism's insistence that people give up to God "every vestige" of their individual will. See Masha Gessen, *The Future is History: How totalitarianism reclaimed Russia*, Granta, London, 2017.

60 "woke indoctrination": Marilynne Robinson, "Dismantling Iowa", *The New York Review of Books*, 2 November 2023.

60 dismantling labour laws: Economics Policy Institute, Working Economics Blog, 31 May 2023.

61 46 per cent of Republicans: Thomas B. Edsall, "'The seeds had been planted. Trump didn't do it himself'", *The New York Times*, 15 May 2024.

61 Thirty-seven per cent: Prison Policy Initiative, prisonpolicy.org.

62 Hundreds of such statistics: Shearer, "Race and politics".

63 "pure white American race": Erin R. Pineda, "The freedom to dominate", *Dissent*, Winter 2024; Hector Tobar, *The New York Review of Books*, 18 April 2024.

64 so willing to kick the racist can: For Trump's racist history, see Mehdi Hasan, "Donald Trump has been a racist his whole life", *The Intercept*, 15 August 2017.

64 Americans living in areas with increasing ethnic diversity: Edsall, "'The seeds had been planted'".

66 "That's Hitler!": Bannon's reaction is described in Jeremy W. Peters, *Insurgency: How Republicans lost their party and got everything they ever wanted*, Crown, 2022. See *Business Insider*, 9 February 2022.

68 Sixty per cent: Pew Research Center, 7 April 2023.

69 positive view of socialism: Statista, 5 July 2024.

70 no president ever made so much money: See, for example, *The New York Times*, 4 January 2024: "At least $7.8 million from foreign entities while in office" according to evidence released by House Democrats.

70 Big money opposed the New Deal: Nancy McLean, *Democracy in Chains*, Viking, New York, 2017; Jane Mayer, *Dark Money*, Knopf, New York, 2016; Brody Mullins and Luke Mullins, *The Wolves of K Street: The secret history of how big money took over big government*, Simon & Schuster, New York, 2024.

71 "abolish your industry": Justin Gick, "Former President Trump addresses petroleum conference on final day", MSN, 17 May 2024.

74 "to soak in the fervor": Chris Solari, *Detroit Free Press*, 15 July 2024.

76 "very problematic theology": Jason DeRose, "Trump assassination attempt lays bare deep religious divisions in the U.S.", *NPR*, 18 July 2024.

76 put violence back at the centre: Sidney Blumenthal, "To his supporters, Trump is a martyred messiah, resurrected after crucifixion", *The Guardian*, 18 July 2024.

76 *New York Post* helped: Rodney Tiffen, "How Rupert Murdoch helped create a monster", *The Conversation*, 12 August 2024.

78 "a dangerous and fraudulent figure": James Fallows, Substack, 18 July 2024.

80 "serene": Armando Iannucci, "The new race", *The New York Times*, 26 July 2024.

82 "a prolific and sophisticated litigant": This is just a fraction of Trump's legal history. An extensive Wikipedia entry, "Personal and business legal affairs of Donald Trump," offers superabundant support for the judge's opinion.

82 Nancy Pelosi: For Pelosi's role in Biden's resignation, see Rachael Bade, "Pelosi told Biden: You're dragging down Democrats", *Politico*, 17 July 2024; Jill Filipovic, "How Nancy Pelosi got this done", *Slate*, 22 July 2024, and Ezra Klein's interview with Pelosi, *The New York Times*, 9 August 2024.

86 "every media outlet": Lara Bazelon, "Kamala Harris was 'not a progressive prosecutor'", *The New York Times*, 17 June 2019.

86 Instead of waging war: E.J. Dionne, "Harris is beating Trump by transcending him", *The Washington Post*, 11 August 2024.

89 "where the choreographed image": Armando Iannucci, "I created Veep: The real-life version isn't so funny", *The New York Times*, 26 July 2024.

HIGHWAY TO HELL

Correspondence

Lesley Hughes

As I write this response to Joëlle Gergis's essay on the sorry state of climate action, the European Commission's Copernicus Climate Change Service is releasing its latest monthly update on global climate trends – this one for June 2024. The edited highlights of the update are that June this year was warmer globally than any previous June for which records are available; that it's the thirteenth month in a row of monthly records; and that the global average temperature for the period July 2023 to June 2024 was 1.64°C above the 1850–1900 pre-industrial average. Add to this the fact that we have also had fifteen months in a row of record-breaking ocean temperatures.

It's all so depressingly familiar.

As several climate science commentators have noted, we may well look back on 2023 as the year the climate broke, when there seems to have been an abrupt escalation in warming, the magnitude of which was so great that one climate scientist went on record to describe it as "gobsmackingly bananas." As virtually every climate record imaginable was broken, we saw catastrophic fires and deadly heatwaves across the Northern Hemisphere and record low sea ice at the poles – the harbinger of dramatic increases in the rate of sea level rise for millennia to come. António Guterres, secretary-general of the UN, memorably stated that "the era of global warming has ended; the era of global boiling has arrived."

For anyone interested in this greatest threat to humanity but who can't quite come at reading the entire million words of the IPCC's Sixth Assessment Report (and let's face it, who wants to do that?), Gergis's essay on the global and Australian Highway to Hell is a highly readable and meticulously researched primer on all things climate change – the science, the inadequate level of global action to address the growing catastrophe, and the peculiarly Australian take on climate politics.

The essay catalogues the sad list of climate change–fuelled unnatural disasters, globally and here at home: the heatwaves, the megafires, the unprecedented floods, the bleaching of coral reefs, the unmitigated misery of communities. And all this with global warming of far less than the 2°C to which we seem inexorably headed. In Gergis's words, "we are disastrously off-track to decarbonise the world." It's a tough read.

Gergis lays out the convincing case that despite Australia, and indeed the rest of the world, being in great peril, there is a "disturbing lack of awareness" of the magnitude and urgency of what we face. She also tackles the "disastrously slow" progress on a national approach to climate adaptation and notes that even if we get adaptation right, there's a limit. She implores us not to look away.

Gergis does a hatchet job on two of the approaches to climate "action" – offsets, and carbon capture and storage (CCS), both of which create "an illusion of progress" but which in practice simply delay the required rapid move out of fossil fuel–derived energy and the cutting of emissions directly at their source. In relation to CCS, Gergis concludes: "Any sensible person can see that pinning our hopes on expensive, unproven technology that will take decades to work at the scale required is absolute madness."

It's worth repeating that phrase "sensible person." Because therein lies the climate conundrum at the core of Gergis's essay.

We've known about the greenhouse effect for 200 years (thank you, Joseph Fourier). The positive relationship between the level of carbon dioxide in the atmosphere and global temperatures was described by Eunice Newton Foote back in 1856. The UN's IPCC has produced six massive assessments, about one every seven years since 1990, synthesising the science, the impacts and the solutions – literally tens of millions of words – and picked up a shared Nobel Peace Prize for its efforts in 2007. In 2023 alone, more than 60,000 scientific papers containing the words "climate change" were published.

Thus we, the sensible people, stand at a moment in human history when our knowledge of the most critical threat to our existence has never been greater. And yet, and yet …

One would certainly like to believe, the madness of the United States aside, that sensible people in a democracy make relatively sensible decisions at the ballot box. In terms of climate action, the outcome of the last federal election came, for many of us, as a great relief. In the first sitting week of parliament the new prime minister promised to "end the climate wars" (though clearly the leader of the Opposition failed to get that particular memo). Gergis gives some credit to the Albanese government for policies such as legislating a somewhat more ambitious emissions reduction target for 2030 – 43 per cent compared to the 26 per cent of the previous lot. There's also the target of having 82 per cent of our energy produced by renewables by 2030, of setting up the Net Zero Economy Agency, of expanding the Capacity Investment Scheme and of creating a National Reconstruction Fund. But at the same time, we see that cognitive dissonance in this government, in relation to climate action, is rife. For every Chris Bowen busting a gut to roll out renewables, we have, in the same cabinet, a Madeleine King proclaiming that Australia will need fossil fuels (gas) for energy "to 2050 and beyond." The Australian Conservation Foundation estimates that the government has approved or otherwise supported sixteen new fossil-fuel projects since coming to office, representing nearly 7 billion tonnes of carbon pollution over the projects' lifetimes. For the foreseeable future, Australia seems set to remain the third-highest exporter of fossil fuels in the world.

Thus far, even the most generous report card for this government would probably be about a C minus – improving, but could do much, much better.

Later this year, the good folks at the United Nations Framework Convention on Climate Change (UNFCCC) will announce the host for the 31st Conference of the Parties (COP), to take place in 2026. Perhaps not as glamorous or anticipated an announcement as that for the next Olympics, the COP nonetheless represents the largest gathering of world leaders in any year. Notable COPs in the past resulted in significant international frameworks for climate action, such as the Kyoto Protocol (1997) and the Paris Agreement (2015). Australia, in partnership with Pacific nations, is bidding to host COP31, with Turkey our only serious competitor.

Would a successful Australia-hosted COP finally rehabilitate our longheld reputation as a climate laggard, a country with, in Gergis's words, a "long and chequered history of delay and denial"? We've got a lot of ground to make up.

Every year, the independent non-profit organisation Germanwatch, dedicated to lobbying for human rights and sustainable development, publishes the Climate Change Performance Index (CCPI), a standardised framework for comparing the climate performance of sixty-three countries and the EU, entities collectively responsible for more than 90 per cent of global emissions. Performance is assessed across four categories: greenhouse gas emissions, renewable energy, energy use and climate policy. For the past decade, Australia has been ranked between 54 and 60, with our performance rated consistently as "very poor/very low." This year we scrambled up to rank 50, shifting from "very low" to the heady heights of "low." Of note is that over the past thirteen years Denmark has received the top rank seven times. Memo to Mr Dutton: Denmark does not have, and has never had, nuclear power.

Reflecting on these results, I can't help wondering if we could all save a lot of angst and millions of well-intentioned words (including mine) and simply cut to the chase – every time a climate-related decision is to be made, we could just ask, "What would the sensible people of Denmark do?"

Perhaps Our (Queen) Mary could stop by and give us some advice next time she's here on holidays.

Lesley Hughes

HIGHWAY
TO HELL

Correspondence

Clive Hamilton

In 2009 I travelled to Oxford to attend a scientific conference titled "4 Degrees and Beyond." It was the first time climate scientists had come together to consider that horrible prospect, which some felt even then was unavoidable. Speaking at the opening, one of the conference organisers admitted that they were worried they would be accused of alarmism by even raising the prospect of 4°C. Those who spoke at the conference were in the vanguard of the scientific community. The army has caught up; the evidentiary basis for their worst fears is now overwhelming.

What interested me most, as the Oxford conference unfolded, were the conversations in the coffee breaks, during unguarded and unquotable moments. The scientists were afraid; they had bad dreams; they did not know what to say to their children (although their children picked it up anyway).

I wrote about the Oxford conference in my book *Requiem for a Species*, published in February 2010. It was met with studied indifference by most climate activists but embraced by a few who were ready to face the facts. In the preface, I wrote of the relief I felt at finally admitting to myself the full truth of what the science was telling me and at no longer needing to devote energy to sustaining false hopes.

Over the years since then I have met quite a few climate scientists who have confessed their deep fears for the future, their despair and depression and the strategies they use to protect their mental equilibrium. A few I've known have been unable to regulate their despair, rushing out into the public square to grab the world by the lapels, shaking it hard and shouting, "Don't you realise what is happening? Listen to us! WE MUST ACT NOW."

Joëlle Gergis's *Highway to Hell* is in this tradition. She begins by telling us she is breaking her silence and speaking out because most Australians just don't get it. She is the expert with the painful truth that we all need to know. The truth, she writes, is "often technical and overwhelming," but don't worry, she will keep things clear and simple. "Please, don't look away," she enjoins us. "There isn't a moment to waste." The trouble is that, at my guess, nine out of ten readers of the essay have not been looking away. On the contrary, they have been watching the scientists' warnings all too intently.

The essay is in fact a shorter version of Gergis's 2022 book *Humanity's Moment*, which took the form of a raw confessional. As David Karoly wrote in an endorsement, "The pages are stained with the author's tears, hopes, heart and soul." Rather than a confessional tone, the Quarterly Essay is fired by a new determination: she has decided to DO SOMETHING.

Gergis tells us she's resigned from her academic job to devote herself to alerting the world to the perils of a heating planet. I admire her for making that move; too few put their money where their mouth is. Perhaps she should have a chat with the formidable, even heroic, Graeme Pearman, who was in effect fired from his job as chief climate scientist at the CSIRO in 2005 because he would not obey gag orders from his "frightened" superiors.

Throughout the essay, Gergis often prefaces expressions of opinion with the phrases "as a scientist" and "as a lead IPCC author." (There were 234 IPCC lead authors.) Gergis is an unwitting adherent to the information deficit model of social change. According to this model, we are in this mess because the public and, more particularly, the important decision makers suffer from an information deficit. If the deficit can be filled with the facts, then they will move to solve the problem. It's a model based on a particular conception of the human (the one scientists are trained to emulate). When confronted with a dilemma, this human investigates, gathers all the facts and works out how best to proceed on that basis.

Believers in the information deficit model cleave to it despite a large body of empirical evidence in the social science journals disproving it. Human beings do not behave as rational calculators but often behave "irrationally." All too often, we prefer sources consistent with our attitudes, we ignore discomforting information, we focus on other things and we won't look beyond the short term. The behaviour of the model's adherents themselves – their failure to accept the abundant evidence that it doesn't work – itself disproves the information deficit model. Yet the lure of rationality remains the basis of science communication, including this essay. Social scientists now publish articles about why the information deficit model refuses to die.

Even if we set aside the complexity of human motivation, the scope of the relevant information is daunting when it comes to a problem as monstrous as climate change. Gergis obviously has a thorough knowledge of aspects of climate science (no one is expert in all of them), but her knowledge of the energy economy, energy politics and the pattern of greenhouse gas emissions is shaky and leads her to make mistakes. There is one claim, one that underpins her political strategy, that is especially erroneous. She writes:

> What happens at the next federal election [in Australia] really matters. As the third-largest exporter of fossil fuels, what Australia chooses to do over the next five years is critical for the stabilisation of the Earth's climate. We still have a chance to determine how bad things get …

It's hard to think of an assertion about Australia's emissions that is more misleading. Whatever happens at next year's election, it can have no noticeable effect on the Earth's future climate. Australia emits less than 1 per cent of global emissions. Emissions in other countries from burning our fossil-fuel exports account for an additional 2.3 per cent. (This figure is supplied by George Wilkenfeld and contrasts with the 4 per cent figure from the Climate Change Authority used in the essay.)

Let's say the next government were to accelerate the trajectory of domestic emissions reduction to reach "net zero" in 2035. The effect on global emissions would be imperceptible. If it rapidly phased out fossil-fuel exports – which I would support – do we really imagine it would cause a 2.3 per cent decline in global emissions? Our main buyers, Japan, South Korea, China and India, might increase their investments in renewables and nuclear power a little, but mostly they would buy their coal and gas from elsewhere. We should do it, but ending our fossil-fuel exports would matter little for the global climate.

Gergis rejects this argument as the "drug dealer's defence." It is indeed legitimate to accuse those who use a substitution argument to defend *continuing* fossil-fuel exports of using the drug dealer's defence. But I am in favour of ending exports on moral grounds while accepting that doing so will not change the global climate. We should arrest the drug dealer even if another will always move in to supply the customers, so it's not the drug dealer's defence. (There are also good economic reasons for making the clean energy transition, including continued access to markets that price emissions, such as the European Union.)

If Australia, accounting for 1 per cent of global emissions, did have the power to "secure a liveable future" for all, as Gergis believes, imagine the earthly power of China, which accounts for close to 30 per cent of global emissions. Yet our small country looms so large in the author's mind that China gets a free pass in the essay. China is installing renewable energy generation at an unprecedented pace, but its total carbon emissions – the only number that matters for climate change – are flatlining.

The bottom line is that no matter how much Australia's role in heating the planet is blown out of proportion for our own masochistic gratification (a temptation I have succumbed to), what we do today barely registers on the global stage. It's regrettable that Gergis, as a scientist who understands numbers, should make such a mistaken claim, going on to tell her Australian readers that, as voters, "The fate of our world lies in our hands." Such a claim may have had a modicum of truth in 1998 when the Howard government held the world to ransom at the Kyoto conference and in 2002 when it repudiated the Kyoto Protocol, but it doesn't now. Rhetorical flourishes at the end of an essay have their place but claiming that the fate of the world is in our hands is more than misleading; it gives false hope.

I spent years defending climate scientists from attacks by deniers, often platformed by the Murdoch media, arguing that we should listen only to those who have earned the right to be heard through their accumulation of expertise recognised by the profession. It's disconcerting when certain climate scientists with no expertise in economics pontificate on carbon pricing (Gergis is in good company here because James Hansen is one of the worst offenders), or with no training in political science or sociology make declarations about how best to bring about social change. And don't start me on their pop psychology of "giving people hope," advice untainted by knowledge of the long and deep history of research on motivation.

Gergis presents her essay as "a guide to navigating the ethical dilemma we all must face about the future of the nation." She doesn't specify the ethical dilemma, but it seems to be a choice between quickly eliminating *versus* continuing to use fossil fuels. At one point, she notes that there are no climate scientists in the Australian parliament and this is a big problem. "We need more climate scientists with enough time to be involved in the political decisions being made about our future right now." She resigned from her academic job because "the most useful thing" she can do "is to use the time I have left to warn the public." If she fails, then, and here she quotes Plato, we will continue to "live under the rule of fools." As she sees it, it is her duty, "as a climate scientist who understands," to do all she can to enlighten them, saying, "The reality is that most politicians and their advisers do not have a science degree, or even a science education beyond high school. And yet we are entrusting these people with the most important decisions humanity will ever make."

In fact, dozens of these people, with no more than a high school science education, do understand and have been working hard, some for years, for policies to slash emissions. A high school science education is sufficient for any reasonably cluey person to grasp the essential propositions of climate science and to understand the implications for the future. I'm guessing most of the readers of this essay fall into this category. If Gergis were to find herself in parliament, I expect she would discover, after months of tearing her hair out, that the roadblock is not a deficit of information about climate change. And if it were, the presence of an IPCC lead author in the chamber would not shift it.

Gergis is one of the good guys and I'm sorry if my criticisms of the essay sound harsh. I'm guessing that for some readers it was enough to be carried along by the shared sentiments of outrage and despair. Personally, I'm tired of crying into our beers and I'm jaded when late sleepers now demand to know "*Why hasn't anything been done?*" After two decades of research into the psychological, social and political complexities of persuading people to recognise and act on the science of climate change, it's wearying when another scientist comes along convinced that it's only a problem of someone with authority communicating *the facts*. I'd be more energised if Gergis, as an IPCC lead author, had written an essay arguing that it's time for a campaign of industrial sabotage.

Leavening the essay's outrage and despair is a good dollop of wishful thinking. Gergis clings to "hope" like a lifebuoy but, apart from relying on the next election result, she struggles to say what hope looks like. In *Humanity's Moment* she wrote: "what gives me hope comes down to this: there is still so much goodness in humanity." Gergis is on a healing journey: "we must also hold a place in our hearts for healing … open ourselves to our vulnerability and our pain." She finishes the book with: "When we awaken this miraculous potential that exists within us all, we can and will change the world."

The book sold well, I believe, so there is an appetite for this kind of thing. Still, I'm puzzled about the readership for this Quarterly Essay. Perhaps it is aimed at the 10 per cent (as a guess) of readers who don't know it all already. Why would the others read it? Masochism? A desperate search for some kind of hope? Or maybe simply out of a sense of duty, just as I sometimes force myself not to look away when images of starving children appear on the television.

If not in this essay, there is a place where we can find an odd kind of reassurance. We know that we in Australia cannot prevent things from getting bad, although we pray the big emitters will prevent things from becoming very bad indeed. It's out of our control. Yet here in Australia there is an enormous amount we can do, beginning now, to transform the nation so that we are prepared for what is coming, giving ourselves a good chance of surviving and perhaps even living well on a hot Earth.

Clive Hamilton

HIGHWAY
TO HELL

Correspondence

David Pocock

In early June, I hosted a parliamentary launch of *Highway to Hell*. It was an opportunity for Joëlle to come to Parliament House, offer her expertise to federal parliamentarians and answer questions about the essay.

The event was well attended by crossbench members and senators, who were visibly affected by Joëlle's sobering presentation. They asked probing questions not only about the data behind the presentation, the projections and the science but also about how Joëlle keeps going, knowing what she knows. How she holds hope alongside grave fears for our future. Her insights were honest and direct, meticulous and well evidenced.

Aside from the deeply worrying picture of our future in a rapidly changing climate, the thing that struck me most was the absence of members of the major parties. It was a unique opportunity for politicians to learn about our greatest challenge from one of our leading minds, yet only one parliamentarian from a major party attended the event: a solitary Labor backbencher.

I was not the only one who noticed this, and Joëlle was asked which ministers she had met with to discuss her findings and the essay. The answer? None. To me, this lack of engagement is emblematic of a broader disconnect between scientific research, public policy and politics.

I have been a senator for a little over two years now and it still shocks me that public policy is consistently shaped by political considerations ahead of evidence and research. Politicians often ignore scientists and instead give weight to advice from pollsters and political strategists. Often they are not looking for genuine, long-term solutions, but for the next opportunity to back their opponent into a corner.

The result is decisions made for short-term political gain rather than to improve the future we are passing on to our children and future generations. We are not making decisions as though we will be here for a long time.

This means that politicians criticising science should be viewed with a degree of scepticism. In recent months, we have seen increasing politicisation of the science around the nuclear energy debate, with the opposition leader, Peter Dutton, claiming that research from our leading science organisation, CSIRO, is "discredited."

Politicians ignoring or attempting to discredit scientific findings put scientists like Joëlle in a difficult position. Scientists are not interested in polls and wedges and backroom deals. But when decisions are made that are blatantly inconsistent with scientific research, their frustration must weigh heavily on them.

We often hear in public discourse that scientists should let the evidence speak for itself, and that science and politics are like oil and water. In this way of thinking, scientists should stick to the science and leave politics to politicians. It reflects a simplistic model of change in which the role of science in society is viewed linearly: greater scientific certainty leads to the political impetus to act.

If it ever existed, this linear model of social and political progress through scientific advancement has broken down. In reality, there are complex feedbacks between the scientific community, the public and politicians. Unfortunately, this relationship often results in the scientific consensus being ignored or downplayed. Social media further complicates this dynamic, with nuance and detail losing out to quick soundbites and cheap clickbait.

Despite the intricate connections between scientists and policy-makers, scientists who speak out after their findings are ignored are at times attacked by politicians, the media and those with vested interests. In no field is this more pronounced than climate science.

Internationally, climate scientists, including Michael Mann, have been attacked and defamed for publishing peer-reviewed findings about the existential risks of climate change. In Australia, Professor Tim Flannery, a former Australian of the Year, faced vicious criticism and was accused of doing the government's "dirty work of fearmongering." More recently, Joëlle herself has been the subject of abuse. Following a comment in the *Guardian*, she was attacked on social media, to which she responded, "Nothing good can come from attacking scientists – we are speaking up because we care about what's happening to our planet."

Against this backdrop, Joëlle's vulnerable and personal account of the science of climate change in *Highway to Hell* is remarkably brave. Progressive change in Western democracies is often catalysed by brave scientists speaking out in the face of public criticism. The work of Rachel Carson to highlight the danger posed by pesticides such as DDT saved thousands of lives in the face of attacks by the chemical industry. Sir Richard Doll spoke out with courage against the powerful tobacco industry following his landmark research that found a clear and unambiguous link between smoking and lung cancer. An Australian scientist, William McBride, was one of the first to identify and call out the link between thalidomide and birth deformities. There are countless other examples.

The relationship between science and politics is ideally one of informed collaboration, where each domain respects the expertise and limitations of the other. Science should maintain its independence and integrity, free from political interference. Politicians must respect the rigour of the scientific process and allow the scientists to present the evidence uninterrupted by political considerations. Einstein's famous examination of the relationship between science and religion can also be applied to politics. Science without politics is hobbled, politics without science is blind.

Science does not end with research and the submission of findings. In the words of renowned British medical scientist Sir Mark Walport, "Science is not finished until it is communicated." Science communicators are a vital part of our democracy. In the United States, communicators like Carl Sagan and Neil deGrasse Tyson have made substantial contributions to conversations that allow science to feed into public consciousness and flow through to public policy. In the United Kingdom, Brian Cox and Alice Roberts have had similar success. Australians and Australian politicians are increasingly recognising the value of science in forming evidence-based policy.

There are a remarkably small number of federal parliamentarians with science backgrounds. Just fourteen parliamentarians, or 6 per cent of the parliament, studied in the field. Nearly seven times as many parliamentarians studied arts (ninety-four) and nearly four times as many studied law (fifty-two). So it's up to advocates with deep subject matter expertise like Joëlle to champion peer-reviewed scientific research and warn us of the future we're hurtling towards.

We are almost halfway through the critical decade for climate action. It is time for politicians to devote far more attention and policy action towards the scientific evidence, particularly when it paints such a sobering picture of the future we're leaving our kids. This is where *Highway to Hell* is so impactful. Joëlle's writing educates and inspires, making it a valuable contribution to the discourse on climate policy and environmental ethics. We need more essays like this. We need more scientists like Joëlle speaking truth to power.

David Pocock

HIGHWAY
TO HELL

Correspondence

Polly Hemming

Most people with a basic comprehension of the climate crisis have probably attempted to practise a form of mindfulness at some stage. It is one of the few effective tools we have at our disposal allowing us to stare into the abyss each day and endure the many facets of climate grief and unravelling horror in our Instagram feed without being consumed entirely.

One of the foundations of mindfulness is the concept of "beginner's mind." Derived from Zen Buddhism, it is based on the premise that often we see things most clearly when we are not attached to them. There is nothing groundbreaking or new in this concept. It doesn't mean bumbling wide-eyed through the supermarket, caressing onions with childlike wonder, or questioning gravity, or naively soaking up everything the Murdoch media spews out. It is just a nice way of reminding us that when we drop limiting biases and habitual thinking in favour of conscious curiosity, impartiality and flexibility, we can approach, assess and handle situations more objectively. We are less attached to the ideas and outcomes we might otherwise favour or instinctively reject.

The beginner's mindset is fundamental to robust scientific inquiry. Credible conclusions are reached by setting aside bias (or funder interests) and objectively and independently carrying out rigorous analysis of data and all reasonable lines of evidence.

Using this approach, climate scientists have reached the unanimous scientific consensus that human activity has been the cause of consistent global warming since the Industrial Revolution. As Joëlle Gergis's essay illustrates with chest-tightening detail, climate scientists have also predicted with a high level of certainty what the *least bad* impacts of this warming will be.

Of course, scientists are only human. But there is nothing to be gained from, nor comfort to be taken in, reaching such a grim diagnosis or confronting the most inconvenient truths. Even factoring in unconscious bias or preconceptions, especially when dealing with such existential subject matter, the sheer quantity of evidence and sheer number of scientific voices saying the same thing is overwhelming.

According to the Australia Institute's 2023 Climate of the Nation, 78 per cent of Australians think that public policies to address climate change should be based on climate science. However, this doesn't seem to be the case given that Australia's domestic and exported greenhouse gas emissions are increasing and projected to increase further – despite the various emissions reduction and environmental protection laws, schemes, programs and mechanisms implemented by Australian governments over decades.

In fact, Australia's supposed "climate policies" are complicated, technocratic, expensive and wholly opaque, designed to distract from, or facilitate, the expansion of the gas and coal industries – the industries directly driving global heating.

State and federal governments are consistently unable to demonstrate how their policy announcements align with the science or translate to absolute emissions reductions. The work of Australia's notional "independent" climate agencies – the Climate Change Authority, the Clean Energy Regulator, even the CSIRO – overwhelmingly reflects the interests of industry, not science.

Despite a rhetorical commitment to climate action by the Albanese government, and the unequivocal advice of the IPCC, the UN and the International Energy Agency that a liveable planet simply cannot accommodate any new fossil-fuel projects, there are more than 100 new gas and coal projects listed as "under development" in Australia, according to official data.

The Albanese government is budgeting for increased fossil-fuel subsidies over the next several years (federal fossil-fuel subsidies alone were $11.8 billion in 2023–24). Policy announcements and legislation indicate the government is also planning to boost fossil-fuel consumption and production in Australia and overseas. The government has recently released a "Future Gas Strategy," which includes plans for new gas basins to be opened despite the strategy itself acknowledging that domestic and global gas demand is dropping.

The terrestrial, aquatic and atmospheric damage caused by these projects will somehow be accounted away by offsetting or capturing a fraction of the billions of tonnes of greenhouse gases they release.

Even without looking through the lens of a beginner's mind, it is clear that what is happening in Australia doesn't make sense. Especially considering that the fossil-fuel companies operating in Australia are also an economic liability: they deliver relatively little in public revenue, are not big employers and are predominantly foreign-owned, meaning the record profits they are making go offshore.

Whatever the reasons, a rapid rethink of our approach is clearly needed.

It is not the job of a climate scientist to analyse or develop climate policy. Developing policy is the job of (the hint is in the name) policy-makers. But because our policy-makers – governments, public institutions and regulators – have failed so spectacularly to respond to the unfurling ecosystem collapse they (and we) have been warned about by the scientific community for decades, climate scientists globally have been given no other choice than to become climate policy experts and advocates.

At a time when academics are increasingly being silenced, censored or bought by the fossil-fuel and environmental market interests influencing their institutions (through "partnerships" or direct funding), it is hard enough for academics to present objective research that may go against these interests. Being forced to then wade into a political debate to defend and advocate for their work *after* bad policy has been implemented is a doubly unfair burden.

And while a climate scientist like Joëlle should not have to become an expert in which economic levers and technologies work to reduce absolute greenhouse gas emissions and which don't, we should be grateful that she has. Given that government and media have been consistently unwilling to do so, it is deeply reassuring to have an independent expert not only telling us objectively what is wrong with the Australian government's approach to climate, but also explaining objectively what will fix it. Because who better to audit and assess the efficacy of Australia's climate policies than a scientist? That is to say, who better than someone with a beginner's mindset, free from limiting bias and vested interests, unattached to any outcome, bound only by the laws of physics, to analyse the data meticulously and pursue all reasonable lines of evidence?

It is both infuriating and a relief to know that the policies, mechanisms and technologies required to address the climate crisis already exist. They are not exciting, but they are cost-effective, and they work. And they've been proven to work both in Australia and globally.

Climate policy, while it may not be easy, is in fact very simple. The first step is to stop doing harm. Stop the industries responsible from putting greenhouse gases into the atmosphere, from clearing land, from poisoning the air and our water supply.

Regulation is not a radical idea. Competition, voluntary action and self-regulation can keep industry in line when the stakes are low, but regulation and law become commensurately more important as the stakes are raised. We rely on regulation to ensure the medicines we take are safe. We rely on regulation to ensure that our employers don't put us in dangerous work environments. Regulation to stop industries destroying our literal life support systems is entirely logical.

The Albanese government has banned engineered stone benchtops in Australia based on the direct link between engineered stonework and serious lung disease. There has been no suggestion that this industry should continue on the basis that the dust from the stone will be captured and stored underground sometime in the future once the technology becomes commercially available, or that the health impacts of silicosis could be offset by ensuring other workers are extra-healthy.

And just as climate policy is simple, so too is economics: subsidise what you want more of, tax what you want less of. The government has not suggested that the best way to limit engineered stone benchtops is to subsidise or expand the industry, yet this is exactly the approach it is taking to limiting emissions from the fossil-fuel industry in Australia: subsidising and expanding it.

If the Australian government wants to reduce Australia's emissions as it says, then research shows that a polluter-pays tax, in conjunction with other policies, is the most effective and efficient way to do it. The government is happy to impose heavy taxes on individuals (collecting over $10 billion from tobacco smokers in 2023–24) but seemingly not on multinational gas companies (collecting only $2.5 billion from the petroleum resource rent tax in 2023–24).

The evidence shows that carbon or polluter taxes reduce greenhouse gas emissions at a relatively low economic cost, with most of the revenue being returned to taxpayers. Australia's carbon price (which was not a true tax and only applied to some sectors of the economy, meaning its impact and revenue potential could have been higher) resulted in a decrease in greenhouse gas emissions and electricity prices and generated revenue that was returned to taxpayers.

Sensible, efficient decarbonisation policies overwhelmingly benefit the broader community. They are fairer, healthier and better for the economy. But because they are not lucrative for a handful of industries, or the entourage of consultants, politicians and senior public servants passing through their revolving doors, they are being sabotaged in Australia to this day.

This means that integrity mechanisms that would keep vested interests out of policy-making and governance are just as important to climate policy as economic and technological mechanisms. Whistleblower protections, an independent public service, whole-of-government transparency, freedom to protest, and conflict-of-interest and accountability laws are the foundations of a functioning democracy and robust climate policy.

We can't expect a climate scientist like Joëlle to tackle these issues for us, though. Nor will mindfulness and meditation get us through, even if they help us to see the situation more clearly and take a more measured response.

Democracy doesn't just happen on election day. Every day leading up to, and after, the 2025 federal election is an opportunity to articulate what constitutes a credible, science-based response to the climate crisis in Australia. Putting an end to fossil-fuel subsidies and approvals for fossil-fuel mining and native-forest logging, and implementing integrity mechanisms with actual integrity, are the bare minimum required.

Whether you write a post on social media, contact your local member, or exercise your right to peaceful protest, Joëlle articulated it beautifully: "what happens next is up to all of us."

Polly Hemming

HIGHWAY TO HELL

Correspondence

James Bowen

The "resource curse" concept holds that geophysically wealthy countries often see poor results from exploitation of this wealth. Australia's institutions have traditionally guarded against the worst negative outcomes seen elsewhere. Yet Joëlle Gergis's essay reminds us that future development of Australia's geophysical assets could have particularly stark and, depending on policy choices, wildly varying socio-economic implications both at home and abroad. The central challenge is that Australia and its international partners must, to an unprecedented extent, develop one form of resource abundance at the direct expense of another.

Gergis outlines Australia's past and likely frightening future experience of climate instability. Yet she also outlines Australia's atypically high degree of agency to influence this future trajectory. Australia is currently a world-leading supplier of climate-destabilising fossil fuels and goods made with these. It is also a world-leading supplier, or potential supplier, of numerous mineral inputs to climate-stabilising renewable energy technologies. It is also a potential world-leading supplier of renewable energy resources and goods made with these, such as "green" iron and steel.

Much rests on the future decisions national and international actors make about which combination of Australian resources they utilise. Sustained development of, and trade in, a more climate-destabilising mix of resources will necessarily impede global socio-economic development. More climate-stabilising dynamics would produce far more beneficial results.

The most hopeful thread running through Gergis's essay is around the evolution in local assessments of the relative economic costs and benefits of climate action. Australia's leaders historically saw only downside in curbing our own and our trading partners' emissions. Now, as Gergis notes, Australian climate change and energy minister Chris Bowen feels comfortable describing a global fossil-fuel phaseout as "Australia's economic opportunity." Coalition support for an Australian nuclear energy sector is widely considered a diversionary tactic. Yet it does at least illustrate how the national debate now firmly demands consideration of alternative decarbonisation visions, rather than decarbonisation versus business as usual.

However, numerous obstacles remain in Australia's path to the "renewable energy superpower" status the Labor government is targeting. This concept has already run into challenges from path-dependent thinking, which often seeks a like-for-like replacement for fossil-fuel exports. Australian and partnering governments and industry members have, for example, likely already spent too much time advancing the vision of Australia as a major exporter of renewable-generated hydrogen, which is beset by myriad cost and technical challenges.

Numerous vested interests at home and abroad might also frustrate giving priority to more economically appropriate pursuits. Gergis gives a good account of how its fossil-fuel industry members and government supporters are heavily promoting the likes of coal-to-gas switching, and overreliance on speculative emissions fixes such as carbon capture and storage. The main hope of these efforts is not minimising emissions but minimising stranded assets.

Unfortunately, pushback against the renewable superpower concept is not limited to domestic sources. International energy customers have proven particularly powerful proponents of keeping Australia as a fossil-fuel superpower. Japan, most prominently, has leveraged the energy market fallout from Russia's war in Ukraine, and its close geopolitical alignment with Australia, to appeal for Australia to remain a "trusted" provider of coal and gas, seemingly in perpetuity.

Gergis doesn't convey the full troubling nature of Japan's interventions in this regard. Japanese critics have clearly argued that any moves by Australia to reduce its fossil-fuel supply would directly jeopardise their country's energy security. Yet, on gas at least, recent analysis supports a view that Japanese companies are mostly interested in Australian resources supplying new markets these same Japanese companies are developing, with heavy state support, in areas such as Southeast Asia.

The uncomfortable truth is that many of Australia's international partners continue to see more of their own economic opportunity as lying in sustained fossil-fuel use. Those who argue Australia must continue to make concessions to Japanese and other Asian demands for fossil-fuel security, to help attract foreign investment in national green endeavours – and there are many – may be either disingenuous or set for considerable disappointment.

Interests and actors tied to Australia's fossil-fuel wealth might forever find justifications for continued exploitation of these resources. The historical argument for why Australia could not take more meaningful climate action was, after all, that domestic economic interests precluded it. Policy-makers supported this rationale even as it came at significant international strategic cost, including, for example, in relations with the highly emissions-conscious Pacific. Now that Australia's leaders appear to recognise the sizeable domestic economic benefits that improved climate action might deliver, they have been presented with fresh, international strategic reasons for not proceeding.

Another worrying development not fully captured in Gergis's essay is the high risk that the renewable superpower vision might itself be co-opted by incumbent fossil-fuel interests. They say that if all you have is a hammer, everything looks like a nail. Australian policy-makers have acquired some new renewable tools. Yet they have retained a very large fossil-fuel hammer. They thus continue to see a lot of imaginary net-zero nails.

Australia's resources minister, Madeleine King, for example, routinely celebrates the supposed role gas and even coal can play in processing the minerals and manufacturing the technologies necessary for renewables deployment. She also notes the role of gas in backing up intermittent wind and solar power. While there is some truth to these arguments, the effect is often to justify massive expansion of supply that is not warranted by energy transition-linked demand, and also to forgo options for reducing this demand. State leaders in the key gas jurisdiction Western Australia go even further, in noting their climate "obligation" to get more gas to domestic and international customers. This is at the admitted cost of the state's, and by extension the nation's, consistently rising emissions.

Political rhetoric from the international to state level has neatly aligned with fossil-fuel and carbon-intensive industry positions. It has in turn been backed by Australian policy commitments to sustained use of fossil fuels. Such commitments often go beyond the "all carrots, no sticks" approach – that is, heavily subsidising green economic interests while not penalising brown equivalents – that now dominates international climate policy-making, such as in the US *Inflation Reduction Act*. For its part, Australia still offers significant state support to fossil-fuel and carbon-intensive industries.

Two closely timed 2024 decisions are of particular interest. The federal budget released in May contained a $22.7 billion "Future Made in Australia" support package to develop green industries. Yet it was immediately preceded by a new national Future Gas Strategy. The gas strategy made no new fiscal commitments, but it did signal that Australia would maintain a regulatory environment that welcomed utilisation of gas "to 2050 and beyond." Japan and other Asian countries greeted the document with immediate claims of renewed investment certainty.

In January 2024, the federal Powering the Regions Fund also provided two major steel-related subsidies: $63.2 million to Liberty Steel and a much larger $136.8 million to BlueScope Steel. The Liberty funding was intended to aid development of an electric arc furnace at Whyalla, South Australia, to kickstart green iron and steel activity. BlueScope's allocation will help extend the life of a coal-consuming blast furnace at its Port Kembla, New South Wales, steelworks. BlueScope had already committed to relining its blast furnace instead of investing in viable lower-emissions technology. Its federal funding was, however, still couched in climate-conscious terms. The government said it would ensure continued domestic production of steel used to produce renewable technologies.

Australian policy-makers profess to see no tension between their disparate sets of commitments. They often even present what are clearly brown investments as somehow green. These are obviously flawed positions. Facilitating sustained fossil-fuel use creates inevitable opportunity costs around the allocation of energy demand and capital. This will only delay the achievement of Australia's renewable superpower vision and its important role in mitigating climate change.

Australia's current leaders should still be congratulated on taking the important step of acknowledging that the country should transition from a fossil-fuel to a renewable energy superpower, for both global climate and national economic reasons. Yet doing so at the speed and scale that Joëlle Gergis notes is necessary invites more deliberate choices. Australia must break the resource curse that fossil fuels and carbon-intensive interests are imposing on national and global socioeconomic development. Our domestic policies and international partnerships must give clear priority to one form of geophysical wealth over the other.

James Bowen

Correspondence

Lesley Head

"Just listen to the science" has been a clarion call of climate change action. Swedish activist Greta Thunberg used it in her speeches to the UN and the US Congress. Australian climate scientist Joëlle Gergis describes her decades of frustration at the science of climate change not being taken seriously by politicians, so much so that she resigned her academic job because "no amount of extra scientific knowledge is going to bring about the political change we need." Gergis has provided a sobering update of the climate record books, and of how climate scientists are reacting to the severity of their own findings. She describes a government in thrall to the fossil-fuel industry and ponders what it will take for the Australian populace to exert enough political will to shift the social licence towards stronger action on climate change.

This intense journey experienced by one climate scientist and shared, to her cost, with the wider community raises many issues. I want to discuss one: the often-implicit expectation that "listening" to science involves a relatively straightforward question of rational policy, just requiring sufficient will from voters and their representatives. As we have spent more than twenty years debating, as a community, the science of climate change, it has become clear that the expectation of a neat segue from good climate science to good climate policy would never go unchallenged by those who stood to lose. The idea that we just needed to amass more evidence, or promote it more widely, was itself stoked by those vested interests. For these and other reasons, the "information deficit model," which assumes that gaps between scientists and the public or policy-makers result from a lack of information or knowledge, is now understood as overly simplistic, in issues from climate change to public health. As a large body of social sciences and humanities evidence now tells us, activating the links between science and policy is neither straightforward nor sufficient to the task ahead.

We didn't get here in a straight line. The processes that led to the converging crises of climate change, biodiversity loss and deep social inequality did not emerge from a universal human nature or a ladder of technological evolution on which the inevitable next step is either a renewable green economy or human extinction. Notwithstanding diverse human influences on earth systems extending back into deepest archaeological time, the drivers of our present planetary crises are now clearly traceable to the extractive intensifications of colonial capitalism, starting with the colonisation of the Americas in the long sixteenth century. As historian and geographer Jason Moore has shown, capital accumulation depended, and depends, on what he calls the Four Cheaps: labour power, food, energy and raw materials. Colonies provided new frontiers of cheap labour (slaves, indigenous peoples) and raw materials from appropriated land. (Those of us in the rich world continue this heritage as we outsource much of our ecological impact to the Global South.) But the bills are falling due, not least in the response of the atmosphere, one of the unpaid-for dumping grounds for toxic waste.

This history helps make sense of the green gaslighting going on as capitalism runs out of Cheaps. Governments – including the present federal one that promised much on the climate change front – and companies perform a mode of action that does not solve the underlying problems but instead facilitates the maintenance of business as usual. Fossil-fuel interests appear to have a chokehold on Canberra and, as Gergis outlines, on the United Nations' COP process. The only actions imagined as realistic and possible are those that do not interrupt the business of economic growth. The increasing criminalisation of protest is a particularly chilling development, allegedly justified because protests disrupt everyday life and people going about their legitimate business.

Although the future looks horrific, Gergis makes the necessary energy transition sound relatively straightforward. We know what we have to do. We have to put the brakes on industrial emissions immediately. We cannot approve new coal, oil and gas extraction. We have to effect a society-wide transition to renewable energy. While we know much of what we need to do from a technological standpoint, we don't know everything. In its 2021 *Australian Energy Transition Research Plan*, the Australian Council of Learned Academies identified "significant gaps in research on the social aspects of the energy transition." There is a lot of work going into thinking about what a just transition will look like. How do we ensure it redresses rather than deepens existing inequalities, particularly for First Nations Australians, rural communities and the working poor? A too narrowly scientific and technological version of the future would deliver a green energy transition and leave everything else the same. This would not fix the underlying problems.

It's not that policy is not important, especially in big society-wide shifts like the energy transition. But the policy tools of modernity, many of which are designed to stabilise business as usual, will not on their own solve a crisis of modernity. What they are trying to stabilise is an economy organised around endless GDP growth; this is what we must change. As the climate scientist Kevin Anderson puts it, there are no non-radical futures. Either we manage to stay within the 1.5°C to 2°C of global warming already in train, necessitating rapid and radical changes in Minority World lifestyles. Or Earth changes for us.

As Gergis identified in her book *Humanity's Moment*, we need to expand our thinking beyond policy and "redefine the cultural and social norms that are destroying life on earth." She and Thunberg embody this redefinition in their work. Thunberg's considerable power lies not in getting people to "just listen to the science"; rather, it is in getting millions of her generation into the streets. Gergis probably underestimates her own power in exposing the emotional dimensions of doing and speaking about climate science. As she discusses in her various writings, dispassion and detachment are strong scientific norms.

Scientific norms have much in common with masculinist ones of strength and optimism, with virtually unlimited capacity to take on challenges and risks. There are many examples of how masculinist perspectives have influenced climate change responses. The "white male effect," in which a range of risks are judged lower by men than women and by white people than people of colour, has increased the level of climate change denial. A broad cultural disposition downplays potentially severe consequences, a phenomenon identified in research as "erring on the side of least drama" (ESLD). Analysis of the responses of senior decision-makers to climate change has identified strong parallels between masculinism, rationality and optimism, in a cultural context characterised by shared norms of positive talk. These norms are shifting as Gergis and other scientists increasingly speak out about their emotional journeys.

Digging deeper into the cultural norms driving our extractive and destructive earth relationships, we can identify the historical trail that frames climate change as an environmental and scientific (thus technological) issue, rather than a social, cultural and geopolitical one. Seeing climate itself as part of an environment separate from humans leaves it stranded "out there," somewhere separated from society, politics, power and culture. That history is embedded in our institutions, laws, policies and scientific endeavours, including environmental ones.

The underlying political struggle in the need to remake the world is well understood, if instinctively, by the fossil-fuel interests that continue to resist change. These interests actively funded the work of climate change denial. Now that denial is no longer tenable, they have shifted to the work of delay. They know how to morph just enough to deflect accountability. They pretend, when it suits them, that this is an apolitical question of objective science. Regular entreaties to "get beyond the politics" or "end the culture wars" on climate change render invisible the deep-seated power structures that benefit from business as usual.

Becoming otherwise can seem an impossible task, even as we know we are living through the end of something. The knotty entanglements of ecological degradation and social inequity can make everything seem even harder. There is frustration, as progress towards a green transition is interrupted by rolling crises – of bushfires, a pandemic, terrible wars on the other side of the planet. There are deep emotional responses we need to articulate and bear. But there is no outside here; addressing the climate change and biodiversity crises is not separable from dealing with the systemic drivers of slow violence.

We won't get out of this in a straight line. But the fact that the task is more radical and more complex than we have imagined does not mean it is less possible. Broadening our thinking beyond policy helps us imagine and mobilise the many kinds of work needed to get traction and leverage on deep social change. Before the window to secure a liveable future closes, we must make the necessary actions thinkable, and enact new worlds.

A lot of this work does not even look like environmental work. It does not have to overtly be work for nature, although that is important too. Everyone who struggles towards a housing system built around safe homes and shelter for all, rather than property investment for some, is contributing towards better climate change adaptation. Everyone who strengthens the public sphere enhances our capacity to act collectively. Not everything needs to look green, and so-called green solutions that facilitate a different set of extractive practices are not solutions at all. The good news is that there is something for everyone to do, and much of it is already being done.

To meet this aura of impossibility, I and many others have taken inspiration from the geographer J.K. Gibson-Graham's work to catalogue the existing alternatives to capitalism. They use inventories of economic difference as a systematic strategy to build "ethical ways of living on our dangerously degraded planet," starting with what we have here at hand. Detailed descriptions and catalogues of already existing diverse labour, transactions and property help destabilise dominant narratives and systems, widening the range of what is possible and what can be imagined. Readers would recognise the important but unpaid care work they already do in these lists.

The task of imagining and enacting the world differently is simultaneously practical and imaginative. We bring worlds into being through combinations of perceptions, everyday practices, narratives, legal instruments, organisations and institutions – all that culture invokes. Australia has an extraordinarily rich set of cultural resources and vernacular capacities – Indigenous, settler-descendant and immigrant – that provide the possibility of doing and being otherwise.

None of this is easy. It may not be quick enough. But our beleaguered climate scientists have enough on their plates. Let's ease some of their burden by broadening how we think about social and cultural change.

Lesley Head

James Bowen is a consultant to NGOs, think tanks and political advisories on Australian and Asian climate and energy matters. He is a former journalist and political speechwriter on resources and energy.

Clive Hamilton is professor of public ethics at Charles Sturt University in Canberra and the author, with George Wilkenfeld, of *Living Hot: Surviving and thriving on a heating planet*.

Lesley Head is Redmond Barry Distinguished Professor Emeritus at the University of Melbourne, where she researches the cultural dimensions of environmental issues, including climate change. She is a member of the ACOLA Steering Committee for the Australian Energy Transition Research Plan.

Polly Hemming is director of the Australia Institute's Climate & Energy program. She was previously a public servant in the federal environment and climate portfolios.

Lesley Hughes is a former IPCC lead author and federal climate commissioner. She is a director and councillor with the Climate Council of Australia and a member of the Climate Change Authority.

David Pocock is an independent senator for the ACT.

Don Watson is the author of two previous Quarterly Essays and many acclaimed books, including *Caledonia Australis*, *Recollections of a Bleeding Heart*, *American Journeys*, *The Bush*, *Watsonia*, *The Story of Australia* and *The Passion of Private White*.

QUARTERLY ESSAY BACK ISSUES

- ☐ **QE 1** *In Denial* by Robert Manne $27.99
- ☐ **QE 2** *Appeasing Jakarta* by John Birmingham $27.99
- ☐ **QE 3** *The Opportunist* by Guy Rundle $27.99
- ☐ **QE 4** *Rabbit Syndrome* by Don Watson $27.99
- ☐ **QE 5** *Girt By Sea* by Mungo MacCallum $27.99
- ☐ **QE 6** *Beyond Belief* by John Button $27.99
- ☐ **QE 7** *Paradise Betrayed* by John Martinkus $27.99
- **QE 8** *Groundswell* by Amanda Lohrey OUT OF STOCK
- ☐ **QE 9** *Beautiful Lies* by Tim Flannery $27.99
- ☐ **QE 10** *Bad Company* by Gideon Haigh $27.99
- ☐ **QE 11** *Whitefella Jump Up* by Germaine Greer $27.99
- ☐ **QE 12** *Made in England* by David Malouf $27.99
- ☐ **QE 13** *Sending Them Home* by Robert Manne with David Corlett $27.99
- ☐ **QE 14** *Mission Impossible* by Paul McGeough $27.99
- ☐ **QE 15** *Latham's World* by Margaret Simons $27.99
- ☐ **QE 16** *Breach of Trust* by Raimond Gaita $27.99
- ☐ **QE 17** *'Kangaroo Court'* by John Hirst $27.99
- ☐ **QE 18** *The Worried Well* by Gail Bell $27.99
- ☐ **QE 19** *Relaxed & Comfortable* by Judith Brett $27.99
- ☐ **QE 20** *A Time for War* by John Birmingham $27.99
- ☐ **QE 21** *What's Left? by Clive Hamilton* $27.99
- ☐ **QE 22** *Voting for Jesus* by Amanda Lohrey $27.99
- ☐ **QE 23** *The History Question* by Inga Clendinnen $27.99
- ☐ **QE 24** *No Fixed Address* by Robyn Davidson $27.99
- ☐ **QE 25** *Bipolar Nation* by Peter Hartcher $27.99
- ☐ **QE 26** *His Master's Voice* by David Marr $27.99
- ☐ **QE 27** *Reaction Time* by Ian Lowe $27.99
- ☐ **QE 28** *Exit Right* by Judith Brett $27.99
- ☐ **QE 29** *Love & Money* by Anne Manne $27.99
- ☐ **QE 30** *Last Drinks* by Paul Toohey $27.99
- ☐ **QE 31** *Now or Never* by Tim Flannery $27.99
- ☐ **QE 32** *American Revolution* by Kate Jennings $27.99
- ☐ **QE 33** *Quarry Vision* by Guy Pearse $27.99
- ☐ **QE 34** *Stop at Nothing* by Annabel Crabb $27.99
- ☐ **QE 35** *Radical Hope* by Noel Pearson $27.99
- ☐ **QE 36** *Australian Story* by Mungo MacCallum $27.99
- ☐ **QE 37** *What's Right?* by Waleed Aly $27.99
- ☐ **QE 38** *Power Trip* by David Marr $27.99
- ☐ **QE 39** *Power Shift* by Hugh White $27.99
- ☐ **QE 40** *Trivial Pursuit* by George Megalogenis $27.99
- ☐ **QE 41** *The Happy Life* by David Malouf $27.99
- ☐ **QE 42** *Fair Share* by Judith Brett $27.99
- ☐ **QE 43** *Bad News* by Robert Manne $27.99
- ☐ **QE 44** *Man-Made World* by Andrew Charlton $27.99
- ☐ **QE 45** *Us and Them* by Anna Krien $27.99
- ☐ **QE 46** *Great Expectations* by Laura Tingle $27.99
- ☐ **QE 47** *Political Animal* by David Marr $27.99
- ☐ **QE 48** *After the Future* by Tim Flannery $27.99
- ☐ **QE 49** *Not Dead Yet* by Mark Latham $27.99
- ☐ **QE 50** *Unfinished Business* by Anna Goldsworthy $27.99
- ☐ **QE 51** *The Prince* by David Marr $27.99
- ☐ **QE 52** *Found in Translation* by Linda Jaivin $27.99
- ☐ **QE 53** *That Sinking Feeling* by Paul Toohey $27.99
- ☐ **QE 54** *Dragon's Tail* by Andrew Charlton $27.99
- ☐ **QE 55** *A Rightful Place* by Noel Pearson $27.99
- ☐ **QE 56** *Clivosaurus* by Guy Rundle $27.99
- ☐ **QE 57** *Dear Life* by Karen Hitchcock $27.99
- ☐ **QE 58** *Blood Year* by David Kilcullen $27.99
- ☐ **QE 59** *Faction Man* by David Marr $27.99
- ☐ **QE 60** *Political Amnesia* by Laura Tingle $27.99
- ☐ **QE 61** *Balancing Act* by George Megalogenis $27.99
- ☐ **QE 62** *Firing Line* by James Brown $27.99
- ☐ **QE 63** *Enemy Within* by Don Watson $27.99
- ☐ **QE 64** *The Australian Dream* by Stan Grant $27.99
- ☐ **QE 65** *The White Queen* by David Marr $27.99
- ☐ **QE 66** *The Long Goodbye* by Anna Krien $27.99
- ☐ **QE 67** *Moral Panic 101* by Benjamin Law $27.99
- ☐ **QE 68** *Without America* by Hugh White $27.99

QUARTERLY ESSAY BACK ISSUES

- ☐ **QE 69** *Moment of Truth* by Mark McKenna $27.99
- ☐ **QE 70** *Dead Right* by Richard Denniss $27.99
- ☐ **QE 71** *Follow the Leader* by Laura Tingle $27.99
- ☐ **QE 72** *Net Loss* by Sebastian Smee $27.99
- ☐ **QE 73** *Australia Fair* by Rebecca Huntley $27.99
- ☐ **QE 74** *The Prosperity Gospel* by Erik Jensen $27.99
- ☐ **QE 75** *Men at Work* by Annabel Crabb $27.99
- ☐ **QE 76** *Red Flag* by Peter Hartcher $27.99
- ☐ **QE 77** *Cry Me a River* by Margaret Simons $27.99
- ☐ **QE 78** *The Coal Curse* by Judith Brett $27.99
- ☐ **QE 79** *The End of Certainty* by Katharine Murphy $27.99
- ☐ **QE 80** *The High Road* by Laura Tingle $27.99
- ☐ **QE 81** *Getting to Zero* by Alan Finkel $27.99
- ☐ **QE 82** *Exit Strategy* by George Megalogenis $27.99
- ☐ **QE 83** *Top Blokes* by Lech Blaine $27.99
- ☐ **QE 84** *The Reckoning* by Jess Hill $27.99
- ☐ **QE 85** *Not Waving, Drowning* by Sarah Krasnostein $27.99
- ☐ **QE 86** *Sleepwalk to War* by Hugh White $27.99
- ☐ **QE 87** *Uncivil Wars* by Waleed Aly & Scott Stephens $27.99
- ☐ **QE 88** *Lone Wolf* by Katharine Murphy $27.99
- ☐ **QE 89** *The Wires That Bind* by Saul Griffith $27.99
- ☐ **QE 90** *Voice of Reason* by Megan Davis $27.99
- ☐ **QE 91** *Lifeboat* by Micheline Lee $27.99
- ☐ **QE 92** *The Great Divide* by Alan Kohler $27.99
- ☐ **QE 93** *Bad Cop* by Lech Blaine $27.99
- ☐ **QE 94** *Highway to Hell* by Joëlle Gergis $27.99

Order back issues online

Prices include GST.
$10 flat-rate shipping within Australia.
Please include this form with delivery and payment details overleaf.
Back issues also available as ebooks from ebook retailers.

WANT THE LATEST FROM QUARTERLY ESSAY?

Subscribe to the Friends of Quarterly Essay email newsletter to share in news, updates, events and special offers.